LONDON'S DOCKLANDS

AN ILLUSTRATED HISTORY

GEOFF MARSHALL

T0322404

First published 2008
This edition published 2018
Reprinted 2023, 2025

The History Press
97 St George's Place,
Cheltenham, Gloucestershire, GL50 3QB
www.thehistorypress.co.uk

© Geoff Marshall, 2008, 2018

The right of Geoff Marshall to be identified as the Author
of this work has been asserted in accordance with the
Copyright, Designs and Patents Act 1988.

All rights reserved. No part of this book may be reprinted
or reproduced or utilised in any form or by any electronic,
mechanical or other means, now known or hereafter invented,
including photocopying and recording, or in any information
storage or retrieval system, without the permission in writing
from the Publishers.

British Library Cataloguing in Publication Data.
A catalogue record for this book is available from the British Library.

ISBN 978 0 7509 8779 0

Typesetting and origination by The History Press
Printed in Italy by Elcograf Spa

CONTENTS

INTRODUCTION

My interest in London's Docklands first arose when I came to London as a student. In some ways the place reminded me of my roots in the industrial Black Country. The atmosphere was one of hard graft, darkness and mystery; life in Shad Thames and Wapping High Street was a world away from that in the West End and the City. From time to time I made journeys of discovery, perhaps a night out at the Prospect of Whitby or The Gun, then an honest boozer for Blackwall dockers, not the smart gastropub it is today. Unfortunately, access to the docks was out of the question, as high walls surrounded them. But now and then, there would be a glimpse of a mighty ship rearing up above the back-to-back houses on the Isle of Dogs.

Now all has changed. The graft and industry have been replaced by the vibrancy of Canary Wharf with its gleaming skyscrapers and fashionable restaurants. But the transformation has worked well. After many early misgivings and scepticisms, the new blends well with the old. It is still possible to walk along Wapping High Street and, with a little imagination, relive life and time as it was between the early nineteenth century when the docks opened and the late twentieth century when they closed.

But what is meant by Docklands? The term was first coined in the 1980s when the London Docklands Development Corporation (LDDC) was set up with the object of regenerating the area. It consisted of 8½ sq. miles of land stretching across parts of the East End boroughs of Southwark, Tower Hamlets and Newham. It began on the north bank of the Thames at Tower Bridge and extended to Beckton; on the south from London Bridge to Greenland Dock in Rotherhithe. This is the area described in this book – even though the term is today increasingly being restricted to modern developments north of the river, centred on Canary Wharf.

Ten years have passed since I published my first book, *London's Docklands, an Illustrated Guide* (The History Press, 2008). This book attempts to describe the area in broader terms, explaining recent developments but with an emphasis on its rich heritage. There are 'What is there to see' sections throughout the book, with a map on page 6 to aid readers. I would like to acknowledge the debt I owe to the many authors who have written about the area before. They are all listed under sources of information. I would also like to thank Tower Hamlets Local History Library, Southwark Local History Library and Newham Local Studies Library from whom I bought images. Images were also taken from Sir Joseph Broodbank's *History of the Port of London* published by Daniel O'Connor in 1921 and still a standard work.

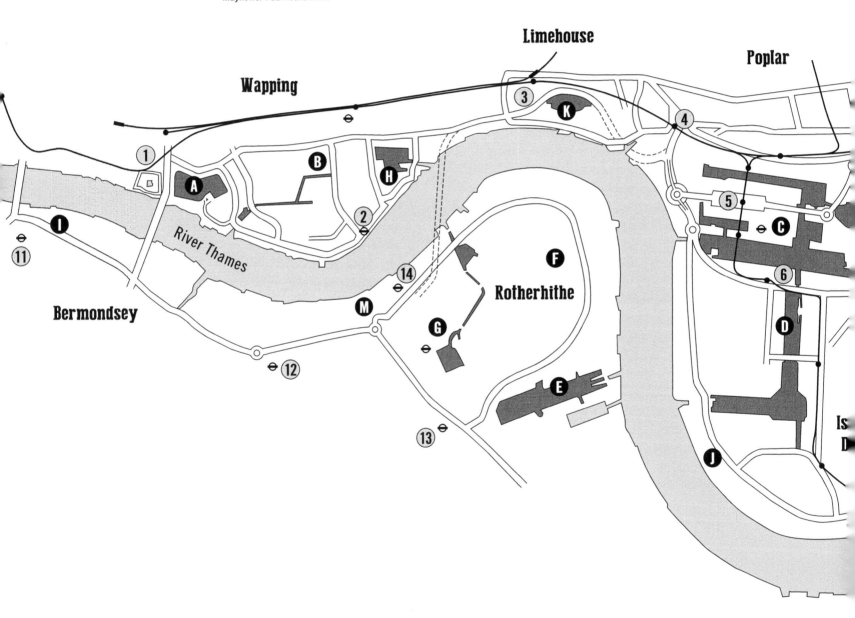

A St Katharine Dock
B Site of London Dock
C West India Dock and Canary Wharf
D Millwall Dock
E Greenland Dock
F Site of Surrey Docks
G Grand Surrey Canal
H Shadwell Basin
I Site of Hay's Wharf
J Great Eastern Launch Site and Site of Millwall Iron Works
K Limehouse Basin
L Island Gardens
M St Mary's Church, Brunel Museum, Mayflower Pub Rotherhithe
N Site of East India Dock
O Royal Victoria Dock
P Royal Albert Dock
Q King George V Dock
R ExCel
S London City Airport
T Emirates Airline Cable Car
U Tate & Lyle
V Trinity Buoy Wharf
W Thames Barrier Park
X Site of Blackwall Yard
Y Site of Thames Iron Works
Z Site of Beckton Gas Works

Wapping

Limehouse

Poplar

River Thames

Bermondsey

Rotherhithe

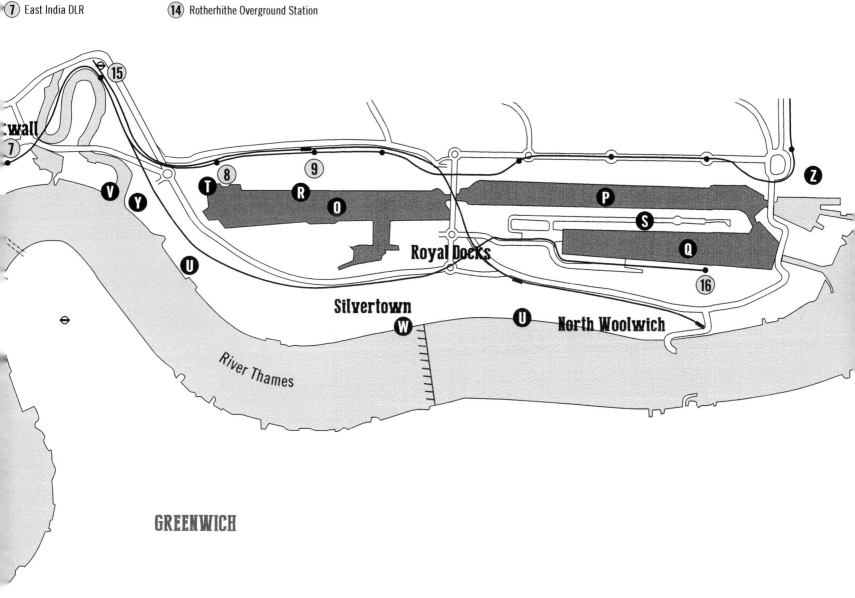

1. Tower Hill Underground Station
2. Wapping Overground Station
3. Limehouse DLR
4. Westferry DLR
5. Canary Wharf DLR
6. South Quay DLR
7. East India DLR

8. Royal Victoria DLR
9. Custom House DLR
10. Island Gardens DLR
11. London Bridge Station
12. Bermondsey Jubilee Line Station
13. Surrey Quays Overground Station
14. Rotherhithe Overground Station

15. Canning Town DLR
16. King George V DLR

wall

Royal Docks

Silvertown

North Woolwich

River Thames

GREENWICH

THE EARLY PORT

The Roman Port

It all started with the Romans. Their newly conquered territory of Britannia lay at the outer edge of their vast empire, and the invaders were quick to realise the attraction of the River Thames as a means of importing and exporting goods as well as gaining access to the hinterland of the country. Founded around AD 50, Londinium became their capital city.

The river the Romans found was markedly different to the river we see today. Recent research has revealed that, contrary to previous thinking, the Thames was tidal in Londinium. It was also considerably wider, varying between about 1km at high tide and 275m at low. The south bank was marshy and often submerged, but the north was well defined, firm with rising land beyond. Londinium consequently grew up and developed on the north bank, the firm land allowing river craft to moor.

The waterfront was about 100m further inland than it is today, and ran along the course of present-day Thames Street. Remains of a Roman harbour were found in the 1820s when London's medieval bridge was demolished. In the 1970s, when the Victorian wharves and warehouses that lined the riverfront were pulled down to make way for the modern riverscape we see today, archaeologists were given a golden opportunity to search for further remains of the Roman port. And their search was fruitful. Research by Gustav Milne and his colleagues at the Museum of London revealed extensive remains of Londinium's Roman harbour, and gave excellent information with which to recreate life in the Roman port.

The archaeological team were fortunate: the Roman timber they unearthed had survived intact because of the absence of oxygen and hence bacteria. Excavations were carried out to the east and west of London Bridge, and revealed a wooden quay west of the bridge, dating from around AD 70, and another, built twenty years later east of the bridge. As a result of the team's work, there is on display at the Museum of London a splendid recreation of Londinium's first-century waterfront, a waterfront that grew rapidly immediately following Boudicca's revolt.

It was not just the Romans' wooden quays and harbour that the archaeology brought to light. In the area close to the wooden bridge spanning the Thames, the remains of Roman warehouses were found. The Roman historian Tacitus has described Londinium as 'an important centre of merchants and merchandise'. By the end of the first century it was the largest town in the province, and the expanding population would have needed increasing amounts of food. Provisions would arrive upstream from the estuary as well as downstream from the farmland to the west.

The Roman citizens would undoubtedly have wanted to retain their Mediterranean way of life and so there would be imports of wine and olive oil from Rome itself. Roman amphorae (storage jars) have been rescued from the mud. Many are engraved with inscriptions telling us of their contents – an amphora has even been discovered complete with its contents of 6,000 olives!

Milne argues that the largest seagoing vessels would not have ventured as far upstream as Londinium because of the unpredictable tides and the treacherous navigation caused by the uncertain and sometimes submerged swamps on the south bank. Instead, imports from Rome would be offloaded at the deep-sea port at Dover and then loaded into smaller ships, better able to navigate to Londinium safely. Roman shipwrecks have been found near the capital, and their sizes confirm this interpretation. In 1910, when County Hall was being built, a round-hulled vessel some 20m long and 5m wide, with a draft of less than 2m, was unearthed. Later, in 1962, a flat-bottomed ship, 16m long and 6m wide, was discovered at Blackfriars. It is fair to assume that the Blackfriars ship is typical of those arriving in London at the time.

By the third century, more frequent hostile raids of barbarians from the mainland of Northern Europe persuaded the Romans to complete the encirclement of their capital with a riverside wall. This structure could not have been favourable to shipping, and therefore it is of little surprise that the port went into decline. Interestingly, recent research by Douglas, in the Highway at Shadwell, has brought to light a large Roman bathhouse and it could be that after the building of the riverside wall the port moved the 2 miles downstream to this site. The bathhouse (second in size to the well-known Huggin Hill baths in the City) was built around AD 240 and was discovered when the American sports bar, Babe Ruth's, was demolished in 2002. It is speculated that the so-called Babe Ruth bathhouse could perhaps have been ancillary buildings to a much larger complex that would have included the relocated port.

By AD 410 the Romans had gone, and next to come were the Saxons.

The Medieval Port

The early Saxons were not a complicated people; their needs were food, shelter and warmth. They were not interested in living in towns, preferring instead to live in small farming communities. So Roman London, including its port, fell into ruin and probably stayed that way for 200 years.

The Saxons settled immediately to the west of the city walls and established a community centred on present-day Covent Garden. It was known as Lundenwic, and, as we are informed by the Venerable Bede, writing in 731, it was 'a mart of many nations resorting to it by sea and land'. But there was no port in the sense we understand today. Milne tells us the mart would have been a very small-scale affair, with trade carried out at the riverside from open boats filled with goods for sale. Boat owners would be required to pay a toll to the king for the privilege of mooring. This sort of market is termed a beach market and, as well as at Lundenwic, there were similar ones at other places such as Greenwich, Chiswick and Woolwich.

The victory of King Alfred over the Danes saw the Saxons abandon Lundenwic for good in the late ninth century and return to the shelter of what was left of the city walls. At first, beach markets continued, but then the waterfront began to be gradually improved by wooden embankments at Billingsgate, Dowgate and Vintry. There were two important hithes (artificial inlets) at Queenhithe and Billingsgate. Queenhithe was originally known as Ethelredshythe, named after King Alfred's son-in-law, and was mentioned in a charter of 899. It later took the name Queenhithe when given to Queen Matilda by her husband, King Henry I.

Following their victory at the Battle of Hastings in 1066, the Normans arrived in London and were quick to improve port facilities by knocking down the Roman riverside wall. In 1176, Peter of Colechurch built the first stone bridge to span the Thames. By 1201, this soon-to-be famous bridge had houses along its length and a chapel at its centre dedicated to St Thomas Becket. The bridge was situated a few yards downstream from the position

View of Billingsgate Dock. (A. Van Haecken, 1736)

Galley Legal Quay, Lower Thames Street, c.1720.

the port, the bridge changed the entire character of London life. There were a total of twenty arches supported by immense piers. The natural flow of the river was severely restricted, and treacherous whirlpools and swirling eddies formed in the water beneath. Under certain conditions, the bridge became a weir. To quote George Borrow, 'truly tremendous was the roar of the descending waters, and the bellow of the tremendous gulfs'. It was common practice, therefore, for ships with cargo bound for quays upstream of the bridge to transfer their goods to lighters downstream and leave it to the skilled watermen to negotiate the bridge.

Despite the impediment of having to navigate the bridge, goods were still landed preferentially at Queenhithe. In 1226, Henry III commanded the Constable of the Tower of London to compel ships of the Cinque Ports to land their corn at Queenhithe, and that all fish was to be confiscated if not sold there. Furthermore, if any foreign vessel unloaded fish at Billingsgate, it should be fined 40 shillings. But for the obvious reason that it was downstream of London Bridge, Billingsgate eventually superseded Queenhithe, and by the seventeenth century Stow described Queenhithe as 'almost forsaken'. While originally landing goods of all kinds, an Act of Parliament in 1699 decreed that 'Billingsgate Market within the City of London shall be every day in the week (except Sunday) a free and open market for all sorts of fish'. The small dock (more an inlet) survived until 1840, when it was filled in to make way for a fish-trading floor.

Merchants from all over the known world came to London; prominent amongst them were the Hansards. The Hanseatic League was a collaboration of merchants from German and Baltic towns (Lubeck, Cologne and Hamburg), established to regulate German merchants operating abroad at so-called *kontore*. In London, the *kontore* was located at the steelyard, on the site of present-day Cannon Street railway station. (The name 'steelyard' derives from the scales used to weigh imported goods.) There were other *kontore* at Hull, Boston and Lynn. The Hansards were granted charters giving them considerable privileges, and when first in London they led a quasi-monastic lifestyle, completely separate

of the present bridge and led into the city where the tower of the church of St Magnus the Martyr now stands. In the centre was a drawbridge to allow shipping through without lowering their masts. Apart from having a significant effect on shipping and

Galley Legal Quay, Lower Thames Street.

from their neighbouring Londoners. They were self-governing, had their own currency, and did not allow members to bring English women onto their property on pain of being expelled from the league. The steelyard had very extensive privileges – 'a testimony to the honesty which the customs authorities found amongst the Germans'. Not surprisingly, their presence was resented by English merchants, which led to Edward VI finally revoking their privileges. Stow tells us 'in the year 1551 ... through complaint of the English merchants, the liberty of the steelyard merchants was seized into the king's hands and so it resteth'. Finally, in 1598, the Privy Council ordered the Lord Mayor and Sheriffs of London to take possession of the steelyard in the name of the Queen and to evict

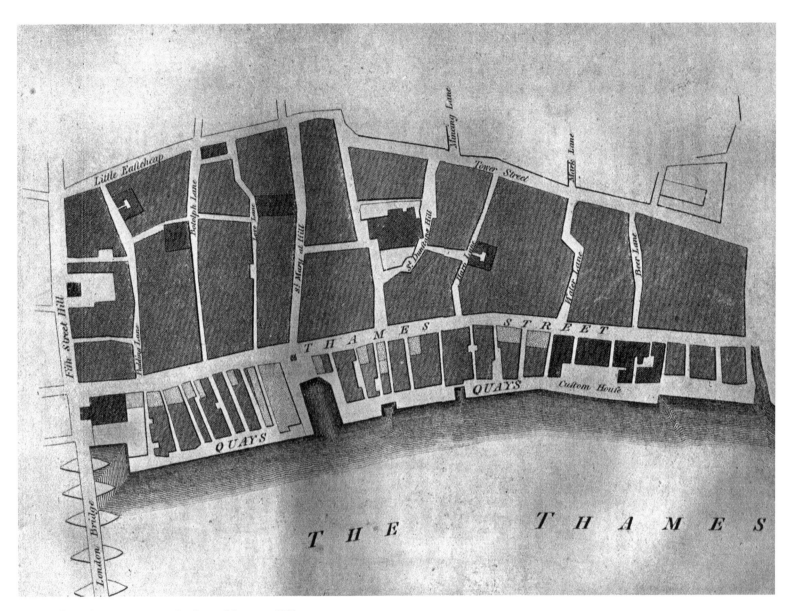

The Legal Quays, from report submitted to House of Commons, 1796.

the Germans from their houses. A few days later, and protesting to the end, the Germans left for good. Their report tells us 'on 4th August we at last left, with gloom in our hearts, the Alderman Henry Langermann in front and we others after him, went out of the door and the door was shut behind us, also we did not want there to pass the night. May God have compassion.' The steelyard was eventually handed over to the Royal Navy.

The reign of Elizabeth I saw the port and trade flourish. It was the era of seaborne exploration. In 1553, Sir Hugh Willoughby set off from Shadwell, hoping to discover the north-east passage to China. The voyage was doomed from the start and Willoughby lost his life in the frozen seas north of Russia. His second-in-command, Richard Chancellor, managed to reach Moscow in safety and there set wheels in motion which led to the founding of a trading company. So was born the Muscovy Company, the first of a series of trading companies founded by merchant adventurers in the late sixteenth century. Sebastian Cabot (the son of the explorer John Cabot) was the first governor, and money was raised from City merchants who subscribed for shares at £25 each. English firearms and cloth were traded for Russian fish oil, furs and timber. Other companies were soon to follow: the Eastland Company trading in the Baltic, the Levant Company trading in the Mediterranean and the Africa Company trading with that continent. But the mightiest of all was the East India Company. It was founded in 1599 when the Lord Mayor of London and City merchants met at Founders' Hall to establish a company to trade with India and the Far East. Elizabeth I granted it a charter, and £72,000 was raised from shares at £25 each. The company's headquarters was at Blackwall and in 1612 they built a shipyard and dry dock there. The East India Company held a monopoly on trade with the Far East for 200 years, and by the end of the eighteenth century wielded vast powers in India. All sorts of exotic goods were imported including pepper, spices, chintz and porcelain.

London's late medieval harbour stretched along the entire length of the City's waterfront. It was lined with wharves which often took their owner's name, or if not, that of the type of cargo handled there. Most goods were subject to customs duty. Corruption was rife and early in the reign of Elizabeth I it was becoming ever clearer that revenues were falling seriously short because of 'greedy persons' – smugglers and corrupt customs officials. Therefore in 1558, an Act of Parliament was passed which decreed that all dutiable goods should henceforth be handled only during the hours of daylight and at specially designated quays, which came to be known as the Legal Quays. They were situated along the north bank of the river between London Bridge and the Tower. Beginning at London Bridge, there was Fresh Wharf and Gaunt's Quay, both landing fish. Then came Cocks Quay, Botolph's Wharf (used by the Muscovy Company), followed by Sommers' Quay and Smart's Quay, both also handling fish. After Billingsgate were Old Thurston's Quay, Dyse Quay and Raff's Quay. Then came Young's Quay, used by Portuguese merchants. Gibson's Quay was used for the import of tin and lead, followed by Sabbe's Quay, Thurston's Quay and Bear Quay. Following on there was Crown Quay, dealing in corn and wood, and Greenberries Quay, finally ending at the Tower with Custom House Quay, Wool Quay and Galley Quay. The names of the quays changed if either their owner or type of goods landed changed.

Wool Quay was long the home of the Custom House. Stow tells us that in the late fourteenth century, a grocer by the name of John Churchman built a house on Wool Wharf that was used to weigh wool – wool being medieval England's chief export. The king gave him certain privileges and permitted him to set up a balance and weights and a counting house there – hence Customer's Quay or the Custom House. It was here, in 1374, that Geoffrey Chaucer, famous for his *Canterbury Tales*, was appointed Comptroller of the Customs and Subsidy of Wools, Skins and Tanned Hides. It was the responsibility of the Custom House to collect both import and export duty. A customs official, known as a 'Tide Waiter', would board an incoming ship at Gravesend and sail with her to her mooring place at the Legal Quays. The vessel's captain would then register his cargo in the 'Long Room' at the Custom House and a 'Landing Waiter' would assess the ship's cargo. It was a complicated business and open to all kinds of abuse.

Compared with the Elizabethan era, the advancement of trade was much slower in the seventeenth century. The Civil War, the Great Plague and the Great Fire of London all combined to make growth more difficult. The Great Fire began in Pudding Lane, close to the port itself, and soon destroyed every warehouse and wharf on the waterfront. The haphazard way in which combustible materials such as brandy, pitch and resins were stored added to the conflagration. After the fire, a tax was levied on the import of coal (one shilling per chaldron) to help pay for the rebuilding of London, and soon warehouses and wharves lined the riverfront once more. It seems lessons were learnt because much stricter building regulations were enforced.

In 1661, a large wet dock of 1½ acres was built at Blackwall, the first wet dock on the Thames, and at the end of the seventeenth century, the Howland Dock was constructed at Rotherhithe. It must be emphasised, however, that their use was restricted to the repair and fitting-out of ships and not the handling of cargo. These two docks are described in more detail in later chapters.

WHAT IS THERE TO SEE?

QUEENHITHE is off Upper Thames Street, 50 yards upstream of Southwark Bridge, nearest station: **Mansion House**.

BILLINGSGATE is in Lower Thames Street, 100 yards downstream of London Bridge, nearest station: **Monument**.

CUSTOM HOUSE is in Lower Thames Street, 100 yards upstream of the Tower of London, nearest station: **Monument**.

CONGESTION, DELAY — 2 THE NEED FOR DOCKS

As the eighteenth century progressed, trade flourished at an ever-increasing rate. Towards the end of the century, it was doubling every thirty years. More and more vessels were entering the river, so much so that it was often described as a 'sea of masts'. But as trade increased, so did congestion and the theft of cargo, and it was against this background that people began to argue for a system of enclosed docks. Chief amongst them were the West India merchants who were losing as much as £500,000 every year from the delay in offloading cargo and from theft. The government also lost money because of unpaid customs duty. Inevitably there were powerful voices in opposition – the owners of the Legal Quays (who had a monopoly) and the City Corporation (often the same people) had vested interests, as did lightermen and watermen. But London was behind the times and needed to catch up with rival ports; Liverpool, for example, had extensive docks by the end of the century and it was inevitable that things could not carry on in the same way as before. Two men emerged to give voice to the general malaise. They were the Dumbarton-born former Lord Provost of Glasgow, Patrick Colquhoun, and the London merchant William Vaughan, both of whom were foremost in urging changes in the way the port operated.

To combat theft, Patrick Colquhoun campaigned vigorously for a river police force and wrote on the subject in his book *A Treatise on the Commerce and Police of the River Thames*. In the stretch of water from London Bridge to Deptford, Colquhoun stated that 879 ships could be comfortably accommodated, but in practice as many as 1,400 were often found. London at the time received ever-increasing amounts of coal from the North-East and so, as well as ships from foreign ports, there were vast numbers of colliers. The figures are impressive. Broodbank tells us that in 1728, of the 8,886 vessels entering the port, 6,837 were colliers. Towards the end of the century, as many as ninety colliers were discharging coal at any one time and each required thirteen barges to carry the coal to its eventual destination. Colquhoun estimated that 1,170 coal-carrying craft would occupy different parts of the port at the same time. As well as coal, over 400 timber-carrying ships arrived every year laden with logs, which, when discharged, were rafted in the river, occupying ten times the space taken by a ship. All dutiable goods had, of course, to be offloaded at the Legal Quays, still situated between London Bridge and the Tower, and offering no more landing room than in Elizabethan days. By an Act of 1663 a series of Sufferance wharves were established for goods of lower value in an attempt to relieve congestion. Five were on the north bank between the Tower and Hermitage in Wapping and eighteen on the Southwark side, giving a total length of 3,676ft. Taken together, the total quay space was only a little over 5,000ft, totally inadequate for the demands put upon it.

The Custom House from the river. (J. Bowles after Maurer, 1753)

The most important import from the West Indies was sugar. Ocean-going vessels would anchor downstream and transfer their cargo to lighters. At any one time, as many as 200 lighters would remain laden with sugar, waiting to gain access to the Legal Quays. Once there, their problems were far from over, for warehousing space was inadequate and only 32,000 hogsheads of sugar could be accommodated. So, in effect, the lighters themselves often acted as temporary warehouses, making them very vulnerable to theft.

Real change in the way the port operated came about because of the endeavours of William Vaughan and his pamphlet *On Wet Docks, Quays and Warehouses for the Port of London, with Hints Respecting Trade*. Vaughan, the son of a London merchant, was born in London in 1752. After education at Warrington Academy under the famous scientist Joseph Priestley, he studied naval architecture at Greenland Dock, and then, at the age of 31, was elected director of the Royal Exchange. He was a fervent free trader and campaigned ceaselessly for improvements in the Port of London and the construction of wet docks. His pamphlet told how:

... the West India trade has been for years labouring under the severest burthens from delays, charges, losses and plunderage ... it is therefore necessary from increased imports and growing impediments to commerce in all its branches, to apply some remedy, and none can be more effectual than the creation of docks and quays, with an extension of warehouses ...

He then compared London's situation with other ports:

Liverpool owes everything to its docks and spirit of enterprise. In 1792 there were no less than 4,403 ships which entered into their docks, producing a dock revenue of £13,243 17s 8d, their ships meeting with immediate dispatch in outfit, loading and discharge.

Vaughan reassured his readers that in London 'situations are to be found on the river, capable of making wet docks of any size' and with a degree of prophecy predicted that 'when one is made, others will follow'. For the first site Vaughan suggested Wapping, which he described as 'an uncultivated waste ... intersected with but few straggling buildings, all of them small ... bad in condition ... and of little value'. He also proposed docks at the Isle of Dogs and Rotherhithe for collier traffic, timber and whalers.

In the same way as Colquhoun was later to argue, Vaughan highlighted the inadequacy of warehousing. 'Lighters are also frequently detained at the quays during a month or six weeks before they are discharged,' he wrote, and continued:

... if Legal Quays are inadequate, their warehouses connected with them are far more so and they can accommodate only about 32,000 hogsheads of sugar at a time and there are not in London spare ranges of public warehouses adequate to the annual importation of sugar alone, at such a period as this, the annual quantity being from 100,000 to 200,000 hogsheads arriving within about three months of the year.

Vaughan expected opposition from people who stood to lose, but countered:

There needs but one general reply to all the apprehensions that may arise from the fear of throwing hands and professions out of employment. Prejudices were once applied against canals, turnpike roads and use of machines in manufacture, but canals have extended old and created new markets without decreasing seamen or the coastal trade; turnpike roads have given improvement to agriculture and convenience to markets and to travellers; machines have given extension to manufactures and we only want docks and quays and warehouses to give facility to commerce.

It was obvious that something had to be done, and to address the problem, the House of Commons established a committee to examine the best way of accommodating London's growing trade and shipping. It called fifty-nine witnesses and reported in 1796. The issues that the committee addressed were those highlighted by Vaughan: congestion in the river with the consequent delays to ships and cargo; plundering; the exactions of wharfingers; and the silting-up of the river. A variety of improvement schemes were considered.

The New Custom House. (From an engraving by R. Havel & Son after a painting by T.S. Roberts, 1816)

The Pool from London Bridge. (W. Parrott, 1841)

A View of the River facing the Tower of London. (W. Daniell, 1804)

The scheme favoured by Vaughan was known as the Merchants' Plan. He proposed a dock at Wapping stretching from Ratcliffe Highway to the waterfront, bounded by Nightingale Lane, New Gravel Lane, Pennington Street and Green Bank. It was planned to extend to 39 acres, hold up to 350 ships and be connected to the river at Blackwall by a canal that cut through the Isle of Dogs. It was costed at £993,000, and its proponents pointed out not just its proximity to the City, but also the time ships would save by not having to sail around the bend in the river at the Isle of Dogs. He suggested other docks in the Isle of Dogs and Rotherhithe for colliers, timber, whalers and light vessels.

The City of London – fearful that its hold on the port was being taken away – put forward an alternative plan, a dock on the Isle of Dogs capable of taking over 400 ships, with a further dock at Rotherhithe, connected to the Grand Surrey canal and reserved for colliers. They also proposed an extension to the Legal Quays by building indented quays perpendicular to the bank into the river, thereby increasing the length of Legal Quays to 4,150ft. Not surprisingly, the latter suggestion was criticised for hindering navigation. The total cost was £1,109,000.

But there were other plans. The architect Samuel Wyatt put forward a scheme for three docks at the Isle of Dogs, but with no warehouses or wharves. Cargo was to be unloaded to floating barges, within which customs men would weigh the goods before transferring them to lighters. Even though Wyatt's scheme offered security to the customs, it was deemed to be inefficient. The cost would have been £840,000.

Southwark was not to be outdone. A plan was proposed for five docks at Rotherhithe for timber and coal, all linked together and connecting with the Thames via an outlet opposite St Paul's. Because its land was cheap and below the high-water mark, the Southwark scheme came out at the lowest cost. It nevertheless gained little support.

Another plan proposed a total of twelve docks, each dedicated to a particular trade. But the most unusual was that put forward by Willey Reveley, who suggested that the river be straightened out by diverting it through a canal between Blackwall and Limehouse. Docks would then be constructed within the existing bend of the river around the Isle of Dogs.

No specific recommendations came from a 1796 parliamentary report, save for an acceptance that wet docks were needed. But the consensus was that they would be built at either Wapping or on the Isle of Dogs; Vaughan favoured Wapping and the former Jamaican planter, Robert Milligan, pressed for the Isle of Dogs. Eventually, in 1797, a Bill providing for docks to be built at Wapping was submitted to Parliament, but opposition and lack of parliamentary time combined to prevent the bill reaching the statute book. Meanwhile, Robert Milligan succeeded in gaining the support of the influential West India merchant, Wharfinger and City Alderman, George Hibbert, for the Isle of Dogs scheme. Accordingly, the West India merchants and the City Corporation began to work together to argue for docks on the Isle of Dogs, mainly because the cost of the Wapping scheme would be too high because of the expense of demolishing houses. They also thought that the more remote site would reduce theft, given that the bulk of pilfering took place upriver. Prolonged discussions ensued over the next couple of years with fierce opposition coming from city porters, watermen, lightermen and the proprietors of the Legal Quays and Sufferance wharves.

Two separate schemes were eventually put before Parliament in the 1799 session. By now opposition had waned, mainly because the proprietors of the Legal Quays had been assured they would be compensated. As the committee minutes indicate, the promoters were now effectively pushing at an open door. George Hibbert appeared for questioning:

Question: Have great inconveniences arisen to the commerce of the Port of London from the confined and crowded state of the Legal Quays?

Hibbert: Very great injury and loss are yearly sustained.

Question: Do you know if many accidents and delays have arisen to loaded ships from the perilous state of the navigation between Blackwall and the Pool?

Hibbert: Frequent accidents have happened to ships of 350 to 500 tone burthen.

Question: Would wet docks (at Isle of Dogs) encourage commerce and give additional security to such trade?

Hibbert: I am convinced (that wet docks) would put an end to the enormous mischief of plundering, which in the West India trade alone has been computed to upwards of £200,000 annually and in which plundering the Revenue is proportionate sufferer.

John Rennie had a similarly easy time when questioned about the Wapping dock:

Question: Would you have any hesitation in undertaking to execute the proposed plan?

Rennie: Not the least.

In the event, it was the Isle of Dogs scheme that, on 12 July 1799, appeared first on the statute book, an 'Act for Rendering More Commodious and for Better Regulating the Port of London'. Its success was mainly due to the City Corporation's interest, and the fact that the West India trade was the most important in the port. The Wapping scheme was to receive Royal assent on 23 May 1800. So were born the West India Dock at the Isle of Dogs and the London Dock at Wapping. Both are described in later chapters, as are all the other docks that followed.

THE RIVER POLICE AND THEFT

Crime on the River

Throughout the eighteenth century, crime was endemic in the Port of London and it was this aspect of the port's operation that most concerned Patrick Colquhoun. Colquhoun spent the early part of his life in Scotland and at the age of 15 travelled to Virginia to familiarise himself with the tobacco trade. On his return to Glasgow, he became a leading merchant, was the first chairman of the Glasgow Chamber of Commerce and rose to some prominence in Glasgow society. In 1792, Colquhoun arrived in London, was appointed a stipendiary magistrate in Shoreditch and began his campaign against crime with his *Treatise on the Police of the Metropolis*. It went to six editions, with crime in the port his major concern.

He identified at least eight different types of thief (or, in his own words, 'species of depredation'), operating on the river, each with their own individual terminology:

♦ River Pirates were nautical vagabonds aided by receivers on the shore. They always selected dark nights for their plunder, having reconnoitred the river during the day.

♦ Night Plunderers were gangs of dissolute watermen working in association with receivers. They would bribe watchmen to tell them which lighter was unguarded and then share the booty.

♦ The Light Horsemen bribed crooked revenue officers so that they could steal as much coffee, sugar and brandy as they could carry away in the dead of night. It was definitely a team effort: The watermen would bring as many boats as needed for the job, the lumpers unloaded the casks from the ship's hold, coopers took out the heads of the barrels and all hands filled the special bags, known as 'black straps', dyed black to conceal them at night. Rum was removed in 'skins and large bladders'. As much as £200 worth of goods could be stolen in one night's work and ships so robbed were termed 'game ships'.

♦ Heavy Horsemen or Day Plunderers were lumpers employed to unload ships. They went to work wearing a sort of underdress called a 'jemmy'. This had pockets before and behind, as well as long narrow pouches lashed to their legs and thighs and concealed beneath wide trousers. Colquhoun tells us that this enabled them to carry off sugar, coffee, cocoa, ginger and pimento.

♦ Journeymen Coopers, employed to repair casks, took opportunities to thieve, as did *game watermen* who offered their services as soon as a ship arrived. Mudlarks were 'grubbers prowling around in the mud under the bow of a ship who received goods thrown overboard by lumpers'.

- Rat Catchers were paid to catch rats on board ship by setting traps for them. They then returned at night and worked hand in hand with crooked lumpers. Colquhoun complained that they 'conveyed rats to the ship to get employment for catching the same animals three or four times over'.
- Game Lightermen concealed part of a boat's cargo in their private lockers.
- But the lowest of the low were the Scuffle Hunters, often called rag-tag and bobtail – casual quayside labourers who 'came with large aprons to conceal their pilfer'.

The River Police

Patrick Colquhoun was to find a kindred spirit in John Harriott. He was born in Essex, the same year as Patrick Colquhoun, and shared Colquhoun's desire to rid the port of crime. Harriot was greatly influenced by his uncle, John Staples, a stipendiary magistrate, well versed in river crime. Under his uncle's prompting, Harriot realised 'the great advantages that would result to all concerned in the shipping commerce of the Port of London if a River Police were established'. He continued, 'I soon formed an outline and consulted my relation who much approved of it.' Patrick Colquhoun also approved of it, as did the West India merchants and the government who put up the money. A river police force was duly established on 2 July 1798 in Wapping High Street, with John Harriott as resident magistrate. This is the oldest police force in the country. It was not uniformly popular, particularly among those whose crimes it had curtailed. A riot broke out when a mob tried to burn the place down, leading to the death of an officer, Gabriel Franks, from a gunshot wound. In 1800, the River Police became a public body and in 1839 it was absorbed into the Metropolitan Police Force as its Thames Division. The present force, now known as the Marine Police Unit of the Metropolitan Police, still operates from the same site in Wapping.

The Ratcliffe Highway Murders

John Harriott was to play a leading part in the investigations into the notorious Ratcliffe Highway murders. In the nineteenth century, the Highway was the scene of some of the worst poverty in the East End. The *Illustrated London News* of 1867 tells us that soup kitchens relieved the distress of more than 1,000 hungry souls each day. It was on the night of 7 December 1811, that the East End witnessed one of the most dreadful murders it had ever known. The scene was the hosiery shop at 29 Ratcliffe Highway, owned by Mr Marr and his family. At midnight, Mr Marr instructed his servant girl, Margaret Jewell, to go out and buy some oysters. She returned about half an hour later, but could not get in because no one would answer the door. Eventually the next-door neighbour, John Murray, a pawnbroker, climbed over the back wall and forced an entry through the back door. He was horrified by what he found. 'The narrow premises so floated with gore that it was hardly possible to escape the pollution of the blood in picking out a path to the front door.' In the back room was a servant boy, James Biggs, whose head was smashed in. Murray then went in search of Mr Marr, only to find him dead in the front shop. Upstairs he found Mrs Marr, who had been suckling her baby. Both mother and child were dead. The baby had its throat cut. Charles Horton, an officer at the River Police Station, was quickly on the scene and discovered a bloodstained shipwright's hammer or maul, inscribed with the letters JP or IP, which he assumed to be the murder weapon. Wapping was gripped with terror and a reward of £50 was offered for the capture of the killer.

Twelve days later there was a second attack at the King's Arms, 81 New Gravel Lane (now Garnet Street). A cry of 'Murder' was heard followed by the sight of John Turner, a lodger at the pub, lowering himself half naked from an upper room with bedsheets tied together. A crowd then forced their way into the pub to find the landlord, John Williamson, his wife Elizabeth and their servant Bridget Anna Harrington lying dead, all with heads split open and throats cut. John Williams, a labourer living at the Pear Tree Inn in Cinnamon Street, was accused of the murders. However, at the time many thought Williams was framed. Before his trial, he hanged himself in the notorious Cold Bath Fields Prison (where now stands the Mount Pleasant Sorting Office). Williams's body was later paraded in a cart in front of the victims' homes, as was the custom of the day.

Billy and Charley

When Shadwell Basin was being built in 1830, it provided an ingenious scam for two illiterate London mudlarks called Billy Smith and Charley Eaton. Billy and Charley became adept at forging medieval medallions by casting them from lead and then claiming they had discovered them in the mud of the new dock. They even went as far as soaking them in acid to give them the appearance of age! Many experts were fooled, and Billy and Charley sold large numbers to an antique dealer in City Road called George Eastwood. The poor mudlarks didn't know that dates in the medieval era were always written as Roman numerals. They inscribed their forgeries with Arabic numerals, a mistake that ended their little game. In time people began to smell a rat and poor George Eastwood was forced to sue those who doubted his integrity for libel. Press coverage gave much publicity, and even though the scam was eventually revealed, the forgeries became antiquities in themselves.

WHAT IS THERE TO SEE?

THE THAMES RIVER POLICE MUSEUM, 98 Wapping High Street, London E1W 2NE. The Museum is open by appointment only. www.thamespolicemusem.org.uk. Turn left for 150 yards from Wapping Station.

BILLY AND CHARLEY'S FORGERIES. There are excellent examples in the **Cuming Museum**, **Southwark**, and the **Victoria & Albert Museum**. For Shadwell Basin, turn right from Wapping Station and right at Wapping Wall for 200 yards to where Wapping Wall becomes Glamis Road.

DOWN BY THE DOCKS

Charles Dickens wrote poetically of 'Down by the Docks' in *The Uncommercial Traveller*. He told of how 'they board seamen at the eating houses, the public houses, the slop shops, the coffee shops, the tally shops,' and how 'the seamen roam in mid street and mid-day, their pockets inside out and their heads no better'.

As we have seen, the West India Dock was London's first enclosed dock built specifically for handling cargo. (Blackwall Dock and Howland Dock predated it, but they were intended solely for the repair and fitting-out of vessels.) The West India Dock opened for business in 1802, and in 1805 so did the London Dock. The following year, the East India Dock was opened. All of these early docks benefited from monopoly rights laid down in their respective Acts of Parliament. The West India Dock had a twenty-one-year monopoly on the handling of all goods either arriving from or sailing to the West Indies, the only exception being tobacco. In a similar way, the London Dock Company had a monopoly on handling all tobacco, rice, wine and brandy, unless from the West or East Indies. The East India Dock Company, always associated with the well-established East India Company, benefited from a twenty-one-year monopoly on cargo carried in all vessels from the East Indies and China. In contrast to the other two dock companies, there were no warehouses at the East India Dock. Instead, goods were carried in heavily secured wagons along the newly opened Commercial Road and then stored in the company's Cutler Street warehouse in the City.

In the early days, with their monopolies in place, the future looked assured for the dock companies. Penalties for breaking the companies' monopolies were severe; the vessel would be seized and a fine of £500 was not uncommon. But there was another clause in all the early Dock Acts which, while not recognised as such at first, was to have far-reaching consequences. It was known as the 'free water clause'. The clause provided for free access to all the docks for all lighters, thus giving them the same privileges as they enjoyed on the river. All other vessels had to pay charges to enter a dock. When the West India Dock was opened, vessels paid 6*s* 8*d* per ton and there were also charges for cargo. Sugar, for instance, was charged at 8*d* per hundredweight.

While the companies' monopolies were intact the free water clause had little effect, but when they came to an end it heralded a new era of competition. Lighters were free to unload ships berthed in any dock and transfer their cargo to riverside wharves or elsewhere. Not only that, they could also load cargo onto ships within the dock system. The Commercial Dock Company was operating on the Surrey side of the river without the benefit of monopoly rights, and consequently they were quick to oppose any extension of monopoly for their neighbours on the north bank. Parliament agreed too, for in 1824 it decreed that ships were free to discharge wherever they wished provided they received customs approval. And this was to be made easier, for an Act of Parliament in 1832 allowed bonded warehouses to be operated by many of the newly opened riverside wharves. As a result, not only were dock companies in competition with each other, but they were now also rivalled by wharfingers.

As the nineteenth century progressed, the port's trade grew, and more docks were built to the south of the river. There was already a ready-made dock on the south bank – the Greenland Dock in Rotherhithe. It was originally used only for ship repair, then became a whaling dock, and was purchased by the newly formed Commercial Dock Company in 1807. Soon to become known as the Surrey Docks, the extensive series of docks in Rotherhithe were to specialise in timber from the Baltic. Then in 1828, the St Katharine Dock opened close to the City, immediately downstream from the Tower of London. By this time the monopolies of the London, West and East India Dock companies had expired. The promoters of the St Katharine scheme hoped to exploit both this and the rush for free trade by building a dock with warehouse facilities close to the merchants of the City.

Meanwhile, the West India Dock Company took over the City Canal that ran between Blackwall Reach and Limehouse Reach, south of the West India Export Dock. The canal was owned by the City Corporation and built soon after the original docks in the hope that shipping would welcome a shortcut through the Isle of Dogs. The canal turned out to be a white elephant, as the inconvenience of having to navigate through two locks resulted in little or no time saving. It was the dock company's intention to convert the canal to a dock, the South West India Dock, a project they eventually completed in the 1870s.

Amalgamations, the Royal Docks and Tilbury

Increasing competition and the effects of the free water clause prompted dock companies to join forces. The East India Dock Company had been badly hit when it lost its trading monopoly with India, and in 1836 the company sold its Cutler Street warehouse to the St Katharine Dock Company. Two years later, the East India Dock Company amalgamated with the West India Company to form the East & West India Dock Company.

The increasing presence of passenger steamships, plying their trade up and down the river, proved to be a hindrance to the operation of the port in the 1830s. Londoners would flock in their thousands to ride on the new steamships down the river to Gravesend and back. What's more, a sport emerged whereby rival ships' captains would race each other, much to the annoyance of working lightermen whose vessels were frequently rammed. At the same time, a further factor added to river congestion. Because of London's increasing population and the proliferation of industrial steam engines, more and more coal was being burnt, and increasing numbers of colliers were arriving in the port.

The figures tell all. 3,871 colliers entered the port in 1792; by 1835, this had increased to 7,980. What amounted to a state of war had broken out between steamships and lightermen, and it was obvious that something had to be done. Previously, the river had been administered by the Navigation Committee of the City of London, but following lobbying by Sir John Hall, Chairman of the St Katharine Dock Company, Parliament eventually constituted the Thames Conservancy Board to regulate river traffic.

Trade boomed in the 1840s and 1850s, and ready to take full advantage were three entrepreneurs: Samuel Morton Peto, Edward Ladd Betts and Thomas Brassey. Unlike the early dock pioneers, they were railwaymen and when they opened the Victoria Dock on the lonely marshes at Plaistow, they made sure it was properly connected to the railways. Cargo could now be transferred rapidly to its final destination; an advantage not lost on the proprietors of the upriver St Katharine and London Docks.

The success of the Victoria Dock prompted the amalgamation of the St Katharine and London Dock Companies; both of which lacked railway facilities and in 1864 they took over the thriving Victoria Dock to form the London & St Katharine Dock Company. On the south bank, the Commercial Dock Company took over the Grand Surrey Canal Company to form the Surrey Commercial Dock Company.

Expansion continued unabated. A new company, the Millwall Freehold Land and Dock Company, was formed to build a new dock on the Isle of Dogs. The Millwall Dock, constructed south of the West India group of docks, was specifically for the import of grain. Then in 1880, the London & St Katharine Company opened the vast Royal Albert Dock, to the east of its renamed Royal Victoria Dock.

In the late 1880s competition grew to such a pitch that, far from being healthy, it was more a case of dog-eat-dog. Disturbed by the success of the Royals, the East & West India Company threw caution to the wind and opened a 56-acre enclosed dock downriver at Tilbury. It had a depth of 33ft, enabling it to accommodate any vessel in existence, and to ease transit of cargo to the outside world there were 50 miles of railway track alongside. Hopes were high, but they proved too optimistic, and within two years the receivers were called in. Between 1888 and 1900 there followed something of a compromise, in which both the London & St Katharine Company and the East & West India Company were run by one joint committee consisting of members drawn from both organisations. Then, in 1901, the companies amalgamated to form the London & India Docks Company.

The Port of London Authority

By now, serious problems in the port's operation had become evident, and in response the government set up a Royal Commission to investigate. Apart from unhealthy competition, there were three major issues that were hindering the port's business. The first was the long-standing free water clause. For many years the companies had campaigned against it, but, not surprisingly, its abolition was opposed by the now-thriving wharves that lined both banks of the river. London, unlike the ports at Liverpool, Glasgow and Hull, was reliant on lighters and many feared that even though London was still the largest port in the world, it could lose its advantage to rival ports both in the UK and Europe. The second factor was that as the nineteenth century progressed, steamships were replacing sail, and by the end of the century they were to predominate. Ships as large as 12,000 tons needed to be turned around quickly, and this was not happening in London.

Port of London Authority Building.

Thirdly, there was the problem with the river itself. The channel in the centre of the Thames was simply too shallow. With a water depth of 33ft, the Royal Albert Dock, for instance, was easily able to take the largest of the new steamers – but even at high tide, the river was only 18ft deep at the entrance lock.

The Royal Commission took evidence from interested parties, including the dock companies, the City Corporation and the London County Council, and concluded that a single authority was needed to run the entire port. However, it was not until 1908, under the prompting of David Lloyd George, that Royal assent was finally granted to the Port of London Act and the Port of London Authority (PLA) was duly founded. The PLA was comprised of twenty-eight members. Eighteen were elected by wharfingers, merchants and shipowners, four from the LCC, two each from the Corporation of London and the Board of Trade, and one each from the Admiralty and Trinity House.

The PLA's powers were considerable. They took over the responsibilities of the Thames Conservancy as well as all the dock companies, but left the riverside wharves in private hands. Furthermore, even though the free water clause remained, all lighters were required to register with the Authority and pay a registration fee. The PLA was empowered to levy tonnage charges on all ships using their facilities as well as charges for cargo carried. There were to be additional charges for the use of its warehouses. Profits were to be used to improve port facilities and the navigability of the river. Work started immediately; repairs began in all the dock systems and new dredging equipment was used to increase the depth of the navigation channel. Office staff were not left out; in 1912, work began on the construction of the PLA's new headquarters on Tower Hill. Sir Edwin Cooper's 'fine building' was opened by Lloyd George in 1922.

Meanwhile the port was completed with the opening, in 1921, of the King George V Dock in North Woolwich, adjacent to the Royal Albert Dock. London's docks were now the largest concentration of impounded water in the world.

WHAT IS THERE TO SEE?

PORT OF LONDON AUTHORITY HEADQUARTERS. The original headquarters were at 10 Trinity Square in a fine building by Sir Edwin Cooper described by Pevsner as 'showy, happily vulgar and extremely impressive'. The building is now a hotel. The PLA is now based in Gravesend.
Nearest station: **Tower Hill**.

WEST INDIA DOCK, POPLAR DOCK AND MILLWALL DOCK

West India Dock

The West India Dock was London's first enclosed dock built specifically for handling cargo. (Blackwall Dock and Howland Dock predated it, but they were intended solely for the repair and fitting-out of vessels.) For reasons of security the Board of Excise insisted that the import dock and export dock be remote from each other with independent entrances from the Thames. The initial plan of the two docks in line therefore had to be changed, with the import dock north of the export dock and the City Canal south of both.

The West India Dock Company was launched as a joint stock company in 1799 with initial capital of £500,000 and a maximum dividend of 10 per cent. There were 353 investors, mainly from the City, West India merchants and planters. George Hibbert was appointed chairman with Robert Milligan his deputy. Ralph Walker was resident engineer and John Rennie acted as a consultant. The chief civil engineer was William Jessop, who had previously built the Grand Union Canal, the vital trade link from London to the Midlands. In 1802, Walker and Jessop fell out and traded 'improper language' which led to Walker's dismissal.

New Docks and Warehouses on Isle of Dogs. (William Daniell, 1802)

The dock was something of a fortress. The West India Dock Act of 1799 required that walls at least 30ft in height should be erected around each dock and be surrounded by ditches filled with water, 12ft wide and 6ft deep. Inside there were sentry boxes and, in the early days, troops. All this was to stop the rampant pilfering that Patrick Colquhoun had written about so vividly, and to ensure that customs revenues were not compromised.

West India Docks, from an aquatint by Bluck after Rowlandson and Pugin.

Foundation Plaque, West India Dock.

The 1803 Warehousing Act enabled certificates to be granted to warehouses to allow them to store bonded goods. At the West India Dock, in place of the 'Legal Quays', a series of bonded warehouses were constructed by the father-and-son team of architects, the Georges Gwilt. Two of these fine warehouses remain to this day, one housing the Museum of Docklands. Their keys were kept jointly by Customs & Excise and the Dock Company. Under this new arrangement, Customs allowed payment to be delayed until the cargo – primarily sugar in the case of the West India Dock – left the secure warehouse for the outside world. As other docks were built, similar arrangements were put in place.

An inscribed plaque describes the laying of the foundation stone of the first warehouse on 12 July 1800, the first anniversary of the West India Dock obtaining royal assent. It was a grand occasion and the excuse for a public holiday. The plaque can be seen at the west end of the range of warehouses. It tells us the stone was laid by the:

> … concurring hands of the Right Honourable Lord Loughborough, Lord High Chancellor of Great Britain, the Right Honourable William Pitt, First Lord Commissioner of His Majesty's Treasury

and Chancellor of His Majesty's Exchequer, George Hibbert Esq the Chairman and Robert Milligan Esq the Deputy Chairman of the West India Dock Company, the two former conspicuous in the Band of those illustrious Statesmen who in either House of Parliament have been zealous to promote, the two latter distinguished among those chosen to direct AN UNDERTAKING which under the favour of GOD shall contribute STABILITY INCREASE and ORNAMENT to BRITISH COMMERCE.

Much of the work was carried out by the partnership of William Adams and the brothers, Alexander and Daniel Robertson who had previously built the Adelphi. It proceeded at a prodigious rate, but the provision of bricks was always a problem, demand outstripping supply.

In 1802, in the presence of Prime Minister Henry Addington, the dock was officially opened with a ceremony during which a ship bearing his name, bedecked with the flags of all nations, sailed into the dock in style. Tens of thousands witnessed the spectacle and *The Times* reported in glowing terms 'of the stupendous scale on which it has been planned', describing the dock as 'appearing like a great lake was an object of beauty and astonishment'. But afterwards it was straight down to business, the *Echo* arriving with the first consignment of sugar. It was the first of many consignments. Ships sailed in through the Blackwall basin to the east. It took them only three or four days to discharge, compared with at least one month when from a berth in the river. Their cargoes were sugar, coffee, rum and mahogany, all offloaded to the magnificent warehouses on the quayside.

The West India Dock had a twenty-one-year monopoly on the handling of all goods either arriving from or sailing to the West Indies, the only exception being tobacco. Penalties for breaking the company's monopoly were severe: the vessel would be seized and a fine of £500 was not uncommon. When the West India Dock opened, vessels had to pay 6s 8d per ton to enter the dock and there were also charges for cargo. Sugar, for instance, was charged at 8d per hundredweight.

West India Dock, showing western entrance and St Anne's Limehouse in background. (Antique print, 1888)

West India Import Dock, 1896.

Work was completed in 1806 and during the company's monopoly trade boomed. In 1804, 254 ships offloaded goods, increasing to 614 in 1810. The company made vast profits; it paid a 10 per cent dividend every year and the value of its stock doubled.

In 1829, the West India Dock Company took over the City Canal that ran between Blackwall Reach and Limehouse Reach, south of the West India Export Dock. The canal was owned by the City Corporation and built soon after the original docks in the hope that shipping would welcome a shortcut through the Isle of Dogs. The canal turned out to be a white elephant, as the inconvenience of having to navigate through two locks resulted in little or no time saving. It was the dock company's intention to convert the canal to a dock with deeper water, the South West India Dock, a project they eventually completed in the 1870s.

When the company's monopoly ran out, it faced severe competition from the East India Dock and the riverside wharves; dividends fell to 6 per cent in 1831 and 4 per cent two years later. Trade improved when the East India Company and the West India Company amalgamated in 1838 to form the East and West India Dock Company. It was a sensible merger; the East India Company was short of warehouse capacity, the West India Company had a surplus.

When the docks were planned, security was paramount – indeed, almost an obsession. The docks had a special police force, and the cottages where the constables lived are still there today in Garford Street. Constructed by John Rennie in 1819, the one in the centre was reserved for the sergeant, while the two semi-detached houses on each side were for his subordinates.

In Hertsmere Road and opposite the West India Quay car park is the Dockmaster's House. Built by the West India Dock Company's resident engineer, Thomas Morris, in 1807, it is in fact erroneously named, and over the years has had many uses. Originally an excise office, in 1846 it was turned into a pub, the Jamaica Tavern. It was later renamed the Jamaica Hotel in an attempt 'to raise the tone'. When the Port of London Authority was created it became the dock manager's office, and then, after the docks closed, it found new life as offices for the LDDC.

When the LDDC was disbanded the building became an Indian restaurant and is now offices of the Jack Petchey Foundation. Sir Jack Petchey, born in 1925, came from a poor East End family and rose to become a successful businessman. He founded the organisation in 1999 and has donated over £100 million to sponsor programmes for the benefit of young people between the ages of 11 and 25. It is interesting to look into the garden to the rear of the building, for the sunken part is a reminder of the ditch that used to surround the outer wall of the dock. The gate piers ahead were the main entrance to the docks from Commercial Road and hence from the City. It was here that the notorious 'call on' took place. In the early days, dockworkers had a small degree of security – full-time workers were taken on at 3s 6d per day – but it was not long before casual work became the norm.

Nearby are more reminders of the strict security that was a feature of the docks. First, there is the PLA police station with its Doric portico. The original police forces of the dock companies were taken under the control of the Port of London Authority in 1909, with a total force for all the docks amounting to 500 men.

In the open space ahead is a Round House, used by the dock's military guard as an armoury for 120 muskets. (The military guard was formed to prevent the docks from being invaded.) Designed by George Gwilt, it once had a neighbour, now long gone, which also served as a lock-up. Rules of early dock life were firm – when a ship entered the dock its crew were forced to leave, and it was left to the company's lumpers (dockers), under strict observation, to unload the ship. Compared with the lawlessness that prevailed when ships lay anchored in the river, and goods vanished almost overnight, the stringent security measures were a success.

The Cannon Workshops, with their impressive central arch of Portland stone by John Rennie, were the site of the dock workshops and stores. They included the cooperage, whose members were elite amongst dockworkers. It was their job to repair barrels and casks. As an added perk, they sometimes had the opportunity to sample the contents! When the dock closed in 1980 the workshops were taken over by small, independent businesses.

Blackwall Basin, West India Dock.

Dock Constables' Cottages.

West India Dock from South East. (W. Parrott)

In front of the Museum of Docklands is a statue of Robert Milligan by Sir Richard Westmacott. It was Milligan who was the main driving force behind the construction of the West India Docks: 'by whose intelligent mind the original plan of this great and useful establishment was designed and to whose admirable perseverance and indefatigable exertions it is principally indebted for the legislative sanction for the arrangement of its business and for its present prosperity.'

There were once nine warehouses, stretching the entire length of the dock. Only two now remain, the others destroyed by bombing in the Second World War. First is the former Ledger Building, designed by the Gwilts. Originally the Dock Office, it was changed to a Ledger Office by Sir John Rennie in 1827 (son of John Rennie Senior) who added the Doric portico. It is now a Wetherspoon's pub. To the left of this was the fire station.

George Gwilt senior was surveyor for the county of Surrey and built bridges – examples including those that span the River Mole at both Leatherhead and Cobham – and set up his son as resident architect. Having won the contract for the warehouses, their brief was that each should hold 8,000 hogsheads of sugar, with basement vaults for rum, and coffee in the attics.

First is Warehouse No. 1. Originally just two storeys in height, it was raised to its present level by Sir John Rennie in 1827. At that time, the monopoly on trade from Asia enjoyed by the East India Dock company was coming to an end, and the West India Dock Company wanted to exploit this by adding further storage capacity. The warehouse was ravaged by fire in 1901, but is now restored to its original form.

Next is Warehouse No. 2, the first of Gwilt's buildings. It has five storeys and is divided into three sections separated by fire walls. Note in particular the cast-iron windows, the lower ones protected by spikes – yet another example of the docks' emphasis on security. Inside, it is possible to see the magnificent cast-iron posts made by the Horseley Iron Company in Tipton, Staffordshire. The warehouse was originally timber-framed, but in 1814 John Rennie persuaded the company to install these iron supports and increase its storage capacity. The magnificent warehouses have now been converted to smart restaurants, with open air seating on the quay. Further along are splendid examples of Stothert and Pitt cranes. The former import dock is crossed by the Future Systems floating footbridge. It can be raised to let boats through and leads to Canary Wharf.

WHAT IS THERE TO SEE?

WEST INDIA IMPORT DOCK AND ASSOCIATED BUILDINGS.
From West India Quay DLR, and looking ahead (west) is the import dock, crossed by the floating footbridge. To the right are the Stothert and Pitt travelling cranes, bonded warehouses (now restaurants, etc.), with the London Museum Docklands towards the far end. Ahead at the end are the Cannon Workshops and the armoury building. Turning sharp right is the inscribed plaque, with PLA Police Station opposite. Left of the gate piers (main entrance to the dock) is the so-called Dockmaster's House and left again in Garford Street, the dock constables' cottages. The import dock is entered from the Thames via the Blackwall Basin, seen from Trafalgar Way (the eastern exit road from Canary Wharf – see Poplar Dock, below) or from Preston's Road (the road, together with Manchester Road, that runs around the east side of the Isle of Dogs).

The South West India Dock (begun as the City Canal) can be seen from the Blue Bridge, where Preston's Road joins Manchester Road.

Poplar Dock

In 1851, the railway came to the docks. The East and West India Dock Company, together with the Birmingham Junction Railway Company, built Poplar Dock, with access to the river via the Blackwall Basin. Previously the site of the dock was used as a reservoir to provide clean make up water to the West India Dock. The railway had the cumbersome name of the East and West India Docks and Birmingham Junction Railway, later shortened to and renamed the North London Railway. The idea was to give access to the dock for manufacturing companies in the Midlands and North via a railway extension from the London and Birmingham Railway at Chalk Farm. Railway construction began from Chalk Farm in 1847 and the dock opened four years later at a cost of £37 million. There was no direct entrance from the river on the insistence of the East and West India Dock Company who were anxious to keep control and avoid any potential competition. Instead, vessels entered via the Blackwall entrance lock and basin.

A deal was reached with the Northumberland and Durham Coal Company, who rented the east side of the dock. Their colliers transferred coal to railway waggons on the quayside for onward transit to north London. This arrangement continued until 1858, when the east quay was taken over by the North London Railway Company. The west and north quay were controlled by the London and North-Western Railway Company to export goods from the Midlands and North including Burton ale, for which a special ale warehouse was constructed. Manufactured goods and iron were also exported.

Other railway companies pressed for export facilities at Poplar and in response a barge dock extension was proposed. It was opposed at first by the East and West India Dock Company, on the grounds that there would be congestion at the Blackwall entrance lock and within the Blackwall Basin. The dock company eventually relented when its South West Dock opened in 1870 with river entrance. The barge dock of 2½ acres was duly built. It was entered from the south of the main Poplar Dock.

Stothert & Pitt Cranes, Poplar Dock.

WHAT IS THERE TO SEE?

POPLAR DOCK. Leave the eastern exit of Canary Wharf Jubilee Line Station, walk ahead to Montgomery Square, turn left into Montgomery Street and at the crossroads, turn right over the bridge and exit the Canary Wharf estate by the vehicular exit, Trafalgar Way. Below on the right is the Blackwall Basin. Turn right at the Traffic Light Tree. Walk along the right-hand side of the road, at the pedestrian crossing turn right into Poplar Dock.

The extension enabled the Great Western Railway, the Great Northern Railway and the London and North-Western Railway to have dock space.

The Poplar Dock was not transferred to the PLA in 1909 and, as a railway facility, remained with the North London Railway Company. Its main business was coal, ale and iron. The dock was devastated by bombing in the Second World War and struggled to survive. The railway lines were removed in 1961 and the dock finally closed in 1981. It is now a marina.

Millwall Dock

Millwall takes its name from the windmills that used to line the wall on the west side of the Isle of Dogs. In 1885, the football club that now plays at the Den in New Cross was founded as Millwall Rovers by a group of workers at Morton's Jam Factory. They were of Scottish descent, hence the club colours of blue and white. They lost their first game 5–0 to Leytonstone, but then went on to achieve a twelve-game unbeaten run. Their first ground was close to the entrance to the Millwall Dock on the west of the Isle of Dogs. It was only in 1910 that they relocated across the river.

Millwall Dock was opened by the Millwall Freehold Land & Dock Company on 14 March 1868, and was originally intended to provide water frontage for manufacturers and shipbuilders, rather than to engage in trade. It is L-shaped, covers some 36 acres with water at a depth of 24 feet and with its original entrance on the west side of the island. At the time, the Millwall entrance lock was the largest in London, with gates operated by hydraulic-powered machinery supplied by W.S. Armstrong and Company. The dock was designed by John Fowler and William Wilson. The company intended to exploit the repeal of the Corn Laws, bringing the possibility of cheap imports of foreign grain. Grain import therefore became, together with timber, the dock's main business.

Millwall Dock. (Courtesy of Graham Thorpe)

Clipper Quay Millwall Graving Dock.

The dock was lined with transit sheds (rather than warehouses, which were for more lengthy storage) and was served by an extension of the London and Blackwall Railway – the Millwall Extension Railway – that ran through to the southern tip of the island to what was then known as North Greenwich. Because of the fear that sparks from steam engines might cause fires, in its early days the rail traffic was hauled by horses. The railway finally closed in 1926; it lost much of its passenger business when Millwall Football Club relocated to New Cross. In 1928, the PLA built the Millwall Passage to give the Millwall Dock water access from the West India Dock.

There were originally plans for six graving docks, to be used for shipbuilding and repair. In the event, only one was built. This was on the site of the Chapel of St Mary, first recorded in 1380 and founded by William of Pontefract. The graving dock was one of the largest on the Thames, 413ft long and 65ft wide. It was leased to a number of concerns, including C.J. Mare of the Millwall Iron Works. The lease was not renewed, Mare being seen as 'undesirable'. The graving dock closed in 1968 and has been replaced by Clippers Quay.

WHAT IS THERE TO SEE?

MILLWALL INNER DOCK can be accessed from South Quay DLR, and the east side walked along to leave by Clippers Quay, the former graving dock, near Mudchute DLR.

6 LONDON DOCK

Plans were made as early as 1793 for a dock in Wapping and near the City of London to handle goods from the West Indies. They were abandoned in favour of what was to become London's first dock, the West India Dock, on the Isle of Dogs. It was left to the London Dock Company (bitter rivals of the West India Dock Company) to resurrect the scheme and begin a dock-building programme in Wapping. Docks at Wapping, 'as near as may be to the City of London and seat of commerce', were seen as a definite advantage.

Daniel Asher Alexander (1768–1846) was appointed chief surveyor and architect. Born in London and a student at the Royal Academy, Alexander was a fine architect, much praised by Sir John Soane for his work at Inigo Jones's Queen's House at Greenwich. In a varied career, he was the surveyor for Trinity House and designed many well-known lighthouses, including that at Lundy. Following his commission at London Dock, as the architect of Dartmoor and Maidstone Prisons, he put his experience of building secure facilities with high walls to good effect. He was much praised by the *Gentleman's Magazine*, who wrote of his work: 'A characteristic fitness of purpose was prominent in every building.' It was, however, John Rennie who did much of the work at London Dock.

John Rennie (1761–1821) was appointed engineer and paid £500 per year. The son of a Scottish farmer, he was educated at the

University of Edinburgh and worked first with mill machinery for Boulton & Watt in Birmingham before setting up his own business in London. Canals were his first interest, and he was also involved with fen drainage. He is best known, however, for dock and bridge building. Apart from his docks in London he also worked at Hull and Liverpool. He designed the former Southwark Bridge and the first Waterloo Bridge – described by the famous Venetian sculptor Antonio Canova as the 'noblest bridge in the world, worth a visit from the remotest corners of the Earth'. His son, Sir John Rennie, completed London Bridge in 1831.

The Bill establishing the London Dock Company received royal assent on 20 June 1800 and work soon began, despite objections from the owners of the legal quays, watermen, lightermen and of course the West India Dock Company. In contrast to the West India Dock, built on the isolated Isle of Dogs, the Wapping scheme necessitated the demolition of houses and the purchase of the Shadwell Water Works for £50,000. The waterworks were built in 1669 to serve East London's expanding population by the speculative builder Thomas Neale, who was also groom porter to King Charles II and builder of much of Covent Garden – hence Neale's Yard. The Shadwell Water Works were built on land Neale leased from the Dean of St Paul's Cathedral, where King Edward VII Memorial Park is now situated. It was at the Shadwell Water Works that Boulton and Watt, in 1778, erected

View of London Dock.
(William Daniell, 1808)

their first steam engine in London for water supply. In 1827, the works were taken over by the East London Waterworks Company.

The foundation stone of London Dock was laid on 26 June 1802, when the 'docks were crowded with genteel persons of both sexes'. The stone was laid by Prime Minister Henry Addington, and within it was a hole in which was placed two bottles of gold, and a trove of silver and copper coins and medals to celebrate King George III's recovery from madness and the Peace of Amiens. To add to the occasion, Lord Hawkesbury, Chancellor of the Exchequer, threw a purse of gold coins onto the stone for the workers to scramble for. The ceremony was repeated at Tobacco Dock and at a warehouse. I often wonder where the treasure is now. Waggons covered with green baize then conveyed the company along Ratcliffe Highway to the London Tavern for 'an excellent dinner' followed by the appropriate toasts.

Construction work was fraught with difficulty. There was a shortage of labour because war with France meant that men either joined the forces or were press-ganged. The company tried to make up for this by employing men to work on Sundays but by so doing fell foul of the Bishop of London and 'The Society for the Suppression of Vice'. The company then resorted to rather more dubious tactics by attempting to bribe the hauliers of the Stepney brickworks, who also supplied bricks for the rival West India Dock, in the hope that bricks could be sent to the London Dock instead, thereby delaying or even preventing work at the West India. The trick didn't work, and the West India Dock was first to open. The first ship sailed into the London Dock on 31 January 1805 at Wapping Pier Head, and the company was then to enjoy a twenty-one-year monopoly on all trade in wine, rice, tobacco and brandy, except that to and from the West and East Indies. Initial rates for ships entering the dock varied from 1s per ton for colliers to 2s 6d for vessels from the East Indies, Persia and China. London Dock closed in 1969. It is now largely filled in, but some buildings survive.

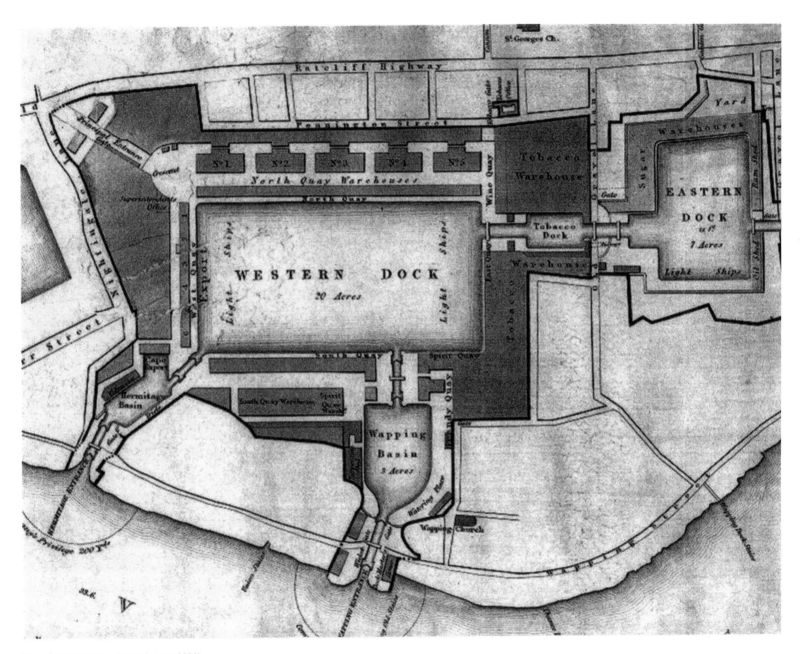

Plan of London Docks. (Henry Palmer, 1831)

Sampling Wine at London Dock, 1896. (Courtesy of Tower Hamlets Local History Library)

There were three entrances from the river. To the west was Hermitage Basin, taking its name from a hermitage that once stood here. It used to be called Swannesnest and in 1370 was occupied by the recluse Friar John Ingram. There was another entrance to London Dock from Wapping Pier Head, converted in the 1960s to a garden. The original dock officials' houses by Daniel Asher Alexander survive on either side; these are now very desirable residences. The end one on the east has a particularly attractive modern extension with uninterrupted river views. To the east is Shadwell Basin. The larger and newer basin to the

New Dock at Wapping. (William Daniell, 1803)

north was constructed in 1858, and the smaller basin to the south in 1832. Before its closure, Shadwell Basin was the main entrance to London Dock; it is now surrounded by pleasant and original housing. They have galleries, porthole windows, arcades and bright colours to reflect the area's Docklands past.

To the north by the Highway and opposite the Church of St George in the East is Tobacco Dock. Opened as the New Tobacco Warehouse in 1814 and now a Grade I listed building, Daniel Asher Alexander's marvellous building, with its roof of timber and cast iron, was quite unique at the time. It epitomises the transition from the timber buildings of the eighteenth century to the iron-roofed structures of the Victorian era. Built by Napoleonic prisoners of war, it had a monopoly on the handling of tobacco, wine and brandy for twenty-one years. The government was quick to appreciate the revenue-raising potential of tobacco, and by 1826, £3.5 million had been taken in duty. Customs duties were paid before despatch. All the imported tobacco was carefully inspected, and any spoilage cut away and burnt on site in a kiln, known locally as the 'Queen's tobacco pipe'.

The warehouse's capacity was huge, capable of holding up to 24,000 hogsheads of tobacco. It covered 80,000sq. ft, with brick vaults beneath. But despite the stringent security of high walls and locked doors, theft was common. Wines and spirits were stored in the vaults below. The aroma in Wapping must have been quite something – tobacco, wines and spirits!

Entrance to London Docks. (Antique print, 1813)

From 1860, Tobacco Dock concentrated on the importation of wool, and became known as the Skin Floor. Sheepskins, with the wool still intact, were imported from Australia, New Zealand and the Falkland Islands and were stacked in huge bales for inspection and auction at the Wool Exchange in Coleman Street in the City. Tobacco importation moved to the giant new Victoria Dock at Plaistow.

Restored and converted by Terry Farrell at the height of the property boom in 1989, it was intended to be a second Covent Garden, with shops, restaurants and historic ships. Plans foundered in the recession of the early 1990s and it is now an events venue. Berthed, rather forlornly, at the entrance are the replica historic ships, *Three Sisters* and *Sea Lark*. They were built by the Hartlepool Ship Restoration Company and transported here by road in sections. They are exact replicas of real ships that would have sailed into London Dock in the early nineteenth century, laden with tobacco from Havana, Virginia or the West Indies.

The original *Three Sisters* was built at Blackwall, but the *Sea Lark* was American, captured by the Royal Navy in an encounter during the war of 1812–14 when she was illegally conveying French passengers and goods to New England.

At the far end of Tobacco Dock is a reminder of one of East London's more unusual shops, Jamrach's Emporium. Here one could purchase the most exotic of wild animals, be they alligators or even an elephant or tiger. There are a couple of statues to recall this unique shop. The one on the left shows a tiger and a boy. The story goes that, one day, one of Jamrach's tigers escaped from the shop, soon to be discovered by an eight-year-old schoolboy. The fearless young lad was foolish enough to stroke the beast's nose, whereupon the tiger picked him up and wandered off down an alley with the poor lad tightly secured in his mouth. Mr Jamrach was soon on the scene, however, and saved the day by thrusting his hand down the animal's throat to release the boy, who walked away unharmed.

WHAT IS THERE TO SEE?

Regrettably, London Dock has been largely filled in to be replaced by Rupert Murdock's 'News International', itself now demolished. There were three entrances from the Thames. The main entrance is at Wapping Pier Head, with the fine Dockmasters' houses next to the Town of Ramsgate pub (turn left from Wapping station and walk along Wapping High Street for 300 yards). There was another entrance at Hermitage Basin: continue for another 300 yards until the junction with St Katharine's Way and Thomas More Street. The eastern entrance is Shadwell Basin, turn right from Wapping Station and right at Wapping Wall for 200 yards to where Wapping Wall becomes Glamis Road.

TOBACCO DOCK and the **HISTORIC SHIPS** are in Wapping Lane. Turn left and immediate right from Wapping Station and walk for 250 yards.

THE EAST INDIA DOCK

There were differences in the East India trade, compared with that from the West Indies. It was controlled by one company (the East India Company) as opposed to the many different West Indian traders. Ships belonging to the East India Company tended to be larger than those of the West India merchants and carried goods of greater value. Therefore, rather than unloading goods in the congested Pool of London, it was the company's practice to transfer their cargoes at Blackwall onto lighters which then continued upstream to offload at the Legal Quays in the City. After customs clearance, cargo would be taken to the company's warehouses in Billiter Street and Cutler Street in the City.

Most theft on the river took place upstream, but following the building of the West India Dock, the East India Company realised they were now vulnerable to the attention of plunderers. Their reasoning was that thieves would come after their cargo now that the West Indian goods were out of reach in the safety of the West India enclosed dock. Pressure therefore mounted for a dock near their ship repair centre at Blackwall to serve the East India trade. In July 1803, the shipowners, Robert Wigram and John Woolmore were successful in persuading Parliament to pass an Act 'for the further improvement of the Port of London, by making Docks and other works at Blackwall for the Accommodation of the East India shipping in the said Port'. The East India Dock Company

was duly founded with Joseph Cotton as chairman and Woolmore as his deputy. £197,000 was raised from 102 subscribers, mainly East India merchants, shipowners and City interests.

There was already a ready-made dock at Blackwall, the Brunswick Dock of John Perry (see *Blackwall Yard*), together with its Mast House, a building used for lifting masts in and out of vessels and stowing sails and rigging. At the time, it was in the hands of John and William Wells. The East India Dock Company purchased it for £35,660, and in 1803 John Rennie and Ralph Walker submitted plans for the East India Dock. Two parallel docks for both export and import trade were proposed, with the export dock built on the site of the former Brunswick Dock, which also served as the entrance basin from the Thames. This arrangement of a combined entrance basin and export dock was soon seen as impractical because of the likelihood of congestion. Land to the east of the Brunswick Dock was owned by James Mather and his whale oil extraction concern, and part of it was purchased by the dock company for a separate entrance basin.

Hugh McIntosh was engaged as building contractor, but problems arose almost at once. His labourers heard a rumour that workers digging the London Dock had been impressed into the Royal Navy. Work stopped, and it was only when the men received guarantees from the dock company that they would not be impressed that construction continued. Bricks were made locally from the spoil excavated at the import dock, and also supplied by Joseph Trimmer from his brickworks in Brentford. At £322,608 the total building costs far exceeded the original estimates.

The East India Dock was London's third set of wet docks and had a twenty-one-year monopoly on trade from China and the East Indies. Its cargo was of high value, spices, tea and silks. All measures were taken to guard against theft: loading or unloading was restricted to the hours of daylight, between ten in the morning to three in the afternoon in winter and four in summer; outside of these hours the place was locked and bolted. In the early days, in contrast to its neighbour, the West India Dock, the East India Dock was not lined with warehouses. Instead, the East India Company unloaded its cargoes into 'long, deep chests, closed on every side and padlocked with iron', which were loaded onto horse-drawn covered wagons to be taken with all haste along the newly constructed Commercial Road, which had been paid for by the company, to their splendid warehouses in Cutler Street in the City.

The East India Dock opened on 4 August 1806 with a similarly lavish ceremony to that seen a few years before at the West India Dock. *The Times* reported that 'the Grand Gate on the land side was opened at half past eleven, and one by one, the place was crowded with genteel company'. There was a

A View of the East India Docks. (William Daniell, 1808)

Entrance to East India Docks. (Antique print)

twenty-onc-gun salute and the *Admiral Gardner* was first to enter the dock, flying the flags of all nations, with (pointedly) the French flag flying beneath all others. Don't forget the Battle of Trafalgar had only recently been fought and won. On the ship's quarterdeck was the band of the East India Company, playing 'God save the King' and 'Rule Britannia' with a full chorus sung from all decks. Between 15–20,000 people witnessed the event and it was recorded that 'as such exhibitions are always attractive to female curiosity, it is scarcely necessary to add, that the whole formed a lively *coup d'aile*, richly studded with beauty and elegance'. Afterwards all dignitaries retired for 'an elegant dinner' at the London Tavern, an opulent eating place in Bishopsgate famed for its turtle soup.

In 1827, the East India Dock Company's monopoly rights expired. The company would then have been exposed to competition, in the same way as the West India and London companies, had it not been for the East India Company paying them £28,000 every year for use of its dock and warehouse. But then in 1833, the government passed the 'Government of India Act', which removed all the East India Company's trading monopolies and the 1827 arrangement was brought to a close. This caused a crisis for the East India Dock Company, only alleviated when it combined with the West India Dock Company in 1838 to form the East and West India Dock Company. The East India Dock benefitted from deeper water than the West India Dock and could therefore accommodate larger ships. Export trade grew, as did imports of seed, jute and guano with special sheds built for their storage.

The adjacent Brunswick Wharf became a place for day-trippers. Doctors recommended it as a cure for consumption 'because you can always get a good healthy blow there'. The dock was the terminus of the London and Blackwall Railway, opened in 1840, with George Parker Bidder and George Stephenson as its engineers. As well as ships full of exotic imports, Brunswick Wharf was used by passenger steamers, whose travellers either caught the train to Fenchurch Street or stayed the night at the dockside Brunswick Hotel.

In the twentieth century the East India Dock's trade was typically jute, seed, wheat, wool and tallow but during the Second World War important work was carried out in the Import Dock. It was emptied and used to build concrete sections of the prefabricated 'Mulberry Harbours', which were used as temporary floating ports for the D-Day landings in Normandy. Both Churchill and Montgomery came to the dock in early 1944 with words of encouragement for the dock-turned-construction workers. The Export Dock was badly bombed in the war and was subsequently filled in and replaced by the Brunswick Wharf Power Station, itself now demolished. The docks closed in 1967.

WHAT IS THERE TO SEE?

Apart from the entrance basin (downstream of the new housing development of Virginia Quay), a small ornamental pond, and some surviving dock walls, all traces of the East India Dock have now gone. The entrance basin is now a nature reserve. From East India DLR, walk eastwards along Blackwall Way. Turn left at the roundabout and almost immediately, leading off the next large roundabout (Leamouth Circus) to the right, there is a pedestrian passageway to the Entrance Basin. Inside there are Display Boards that explain what wildlife can be seen.

Opening of West India Docks, the *Henry Addington* decorated with the colours of all nations. (P.O. Tomkins, 1802)

The Custom House, from an engraving by R.G. Reeve, after a painting by S. Owen, 1828.

West India Quay and Gwilts' Warehouses.

West India Import Dock, 2017.

CLOCKWISE FROM ABOVE: Armoury, West India Import Dock; Shadwell Basin, London Dock; Former Main Entrance to London Dock.

Historic Ships, Tobacco Dock.

East India Dock Entrance Basin, 2017.
Note Emirates Airline in background.

Greenland Dock (looking east).

Greenland Dock (looking west).

Lavender Dock Nature Reserve.

St Katharine Dock with Ivory House in background.

Thomas Telford Footbridge at St Katharine Dock.

Royal Victoria Dock.

Shad Thames.

Royal Albert Dock plus University East London housing.

Butler's Wharf.

CLOCKWISE FROM LEFT: St Saviour's Dock; Shad Thames; Trinity Buoy Wharf.

Canary Wharf from Glengall Bridge, Millwall.

Canary Wharf from Millwall Dock.

Canary Wharf from Rotherhithe.

Canary Wharf Jubilee Line station.

Jubilee Park, Canary Wharf.

London City Airport plus King George V Dock.

Royal Mint, Tower Hill. (Courtesy of Tower Hamlets Local History Library)

Greenwich from Island Gardens.

Lyles Golden Syrup.

Limehouse Basin.

Entrance to Regent's Canal and Limehouse Dock (Thomas Shepherd and F.J. Havel, 1828). The building on the left is now replaced by Gordon Ramsay's 'The Narrow'.

CLOCKWISE FROM LEFT: Limehouse Cut; *Rope Circle* by Wendy Taylor, Hermitage Basin; *Dr Salter's Cat* by Diane Gorvin, Bermondsey.

The Town of Ramsgate, Wapping.

The Prospect of Whitby, Wapping.

The Narrow, Limehouse.

The Ledger Building, West India Quay.

The Ship and Whale, Rotherhithe.

The Ferry House, Isle of Dogs.

The Mayflower, Rotherhithe.

THE SURREY DOCKS

The oldest surviving wet dock in London's dock system is the Greenland Dock, opened in 1699 as the Howland Great Wet Dock. When built it was much smaller than it is now, extending some 1,070ft from the riverbank and capable of holding 120 of the largest merchant vessels. The dock came about because of the marriage of 11-year-old Elizabeth Howland to 14-year-old Wriothesley Russell in 1695. These children came from formidable families. The Howlands had connections with the East India Company, and the Russell family held the Dukedom of Bedford. And it was the young couple's recently widowed mothers who influenced the passing of an Act of Parliament in 1696 to enable the dock to be constructed.

It must be emphasised that in its early days the dock wasn't used for handling cargoes, but solely for the fitting-out of vessels and as a safe haven. It was then in a rural setting and surrounded by trees, whose shelter protected the ships within from storm damage. The great storm of 27 November 1703 destroyed the Eddystone Lighthouse and wrecked many ships anchored on the river. Those vessels moored within the newly opened dock, however, were saved.

It is highly probable that the dock was built by John Wells, a member of a famous shipbuilding family. In 1763, the dock, now known as the Greenland Dock, passed to the Wells concern. Greenland Dock is so named because of the whaling trade that was centred on its quayside. In the mid-eighteenth century, the government began to provide financial incentives to encourage the whaling industry. It had the desired effect; in 1753, thirty-five ships left Britain to sail to the waters around Greenland in search of the Greenland right whale, and by 1788 the number had increased to 225, of which ninety-one were from London. Oil from the blubber was used in the manufacture of soap, in paints and varnishes, and, most importantly, it was burnt for domestic lighting. Whaling ships left Greenland Dock every spring and spent the summer months in the Arctic. The Greenland right whale was so named because it was 'the right one to hunt'. It is now more commonly known as the Bowhead whale; they are gigantic animals, measuring around 60ft in length. When harvested in the eighteenth century each one could yield 20 tons of oil. The blubber was cut up on the ship and stored in barrels, ready to be unloaded when the whalers returned to London in the autumn. The dockside was lined with sheds where the blubber was 'tried out'. In this process, the blubber was loaded into 'coppers', each with a capacity of 10 tons, which were heated by a furnace below to extract the oil. The oil was then transferred by ladles to 'fritter barrows', where it was strained to remove sediment. As much as 1,000 tons were boiled annually and the stench was appalling. In *Moby-Dick*, Herman Melville remarked it was like 'excavating an old city graveyard'. Whalebone was

a by-product of the industry and was used for stays, umbrellas and hat frames. Towards the end of the eighteenth century, when whaling ships were built that were capable of extracting oil on board, the whaling trade declined.

Meanwhile, the Surrey Canal Company had been incorporated by an Act of Parliament in May 1801. The Grand Surrey Canal was the idea of Ralph Dodd, an engineer, who obtained powers to construct a canal from Wilkinson's Gun Wharf on the riverside at Rotherhithe to Mitcham in Surrey. Dodd, author of *Account and Principle of Canals in the Known World*, was a man with grand ideas – he once had an ill-fated plan to build a tunnel under the Thames

LEFT: Howland Dock, 1700. Note line of trees on each quay.

BELOW: Commercial Docks, Rotherhithe. (William Daniell, 1813)

between Gravesend and Tilbury. And his plan for the Grand Surrey Canal was similarly ambitious. He planned that it should extend to Epsom in Surrey and even to Portsmouth and the coast. In the event, the proprietors lost interest in Dodd because of his high costs and the project was put out to tender. John Dyson came in with the lowest bid, which was accepted, and Ralph Walker was appointed as engineer. The canal ran for 3½ miles from the Thames at Rotherhithe, through the market gardens of Deptford and Peckham to Camberwell. It was the first canal to have a police force and Bank Rangers, as they were called, were appointed to keep order. It was the proprietors' original intention that the canal would serve to transport market gardeners' produce to the people of London, but the gardens were soon to be swallowed up by the ever-expanding thrust of London itself.

Within a year, Mr John Hall, a wealthy shipowner, looked with envious eyes across the river to witness the dock building that was happening apace on that side of the river and came up with an alternative scheme for the canal. Hall submitted plans for a basin and lock to the Thames and in October 1803, the canal company resolved 'that the entrance basin and lock into the river at Warlter's Wharf be carried into immediate effect'. It was known as the Grand Surrey Basin. Building began in November 1804 and on 13 March 1807 the canal opened with the usual ceremony:

> … in the presence of a numerous assemblage of spectators, composed principally of the proprietors and their friends, together with a large company of ladies, who all appeared much gratified on this interesting occasion … guns were fired as a signal for the first vessel to enter and at 3 o' clock the Argo, dressed in the colours of various nations entered amidst the acclamations of the spectators. She was saluted by a discharge of cannon from the shore which was returned by the vessel; while the band of martial music on the deck played 'God Save the King' and 'Rule Britannia'. The whole made a very interesting appearance.

VIEW OF THE GRAND SURREY DOCKS CANAL

ENTRANCE TO SURREY CANAL FROM THAMES

ENTRANCE TO THE COMMERCIAL DOCKS—ROTHERHITHE
From unpublished water-colours by G. Yates, 1825   p. 220

Scenes from the Grand Surrey Canal. (G. Yates, 1825)

To return now to the account of the Greenland Dock, the Commercial Dock Company was formed at a meeting at the London Tavern on 18 September 1807 and at once determined to purchase the Greenland Dock and the adjacent Norway Dock from the current owner, William Ritchie. They paid Ritchie £35,000 and appointed James Walker as their chief engineer, who soon set about rebuilding. It was the Commercial Dock Company's intention to exploit the Baltic timber trade. Accordingly, at the Greenland Dock, whaling was replaced by the import of timber. Two sets of workers were employed, the 'lumpers' and the 'deal porters'. It was the lumpers' job to unload the timber from the ship's hold, and then on the quayside the more highly skilled deal porters took over. By tradition they 'worked hard, drank hard and were too old at forty', but they were expert at their trade. They had to stack timber planks to a height of 50ft or more, and their ability to balance long planks on their shoulders gave them the nickname 'Blondins' after the well-known tightrope walker. They were recognised by their distinctive long leather hats, with flaps designed to protect their shoulders.

Two other companies then entered the fray. First was the Baltic Dock Company. It owned 45 acres of land, north of the Greenland Dock and east of the Grand Surrey Canal, within which it intended to build ponds to store timber and construct an entrance from the river. The company was headed by Joseph Moore who had obtained favourable promises from the government for bonding timber. The Commercial Dock Company quickly realised the threat and bought the Baltic Company, hoping that the promised privileges would pass to them. They were disappointed! Also, in 1807, work began constructing a dock just to the south of the Greenland Dock. It was known as the East Country Dock and it achieved statutory authority in 1811. Like the other companies, the East Country Dock Company dealt in the increasingly profitable timber trade.

In 1825, the Surrey Canal Company revived the ambitious dreams of its founder, Ralph Dodd, and proposed a bold scheme to extend their canal as a ship canal to Portsmouth. Capital of £5 million was needed. The canal was to be tidal with no locks and be 'navigable to ships of the largest size fully equipped and laden'. The 'stupendous national object' as it was described never got off the ground; the coming of the railways intervened. But what a pity; the thought of a ship gliding on a canal through leafy Surrey is rather appealing. By an Act of Parliament of 1855, the canal company changed its name to The Grand Surrey Docks & Canal Company and raised money to build a new dock of 16 acres, known as Albion Dock, which opened in 1860. Four years later, The Grand Surrey Docks & Canal Company merged with the Commercial Dock Company.

In 1850, the Commercial Dock Company had acquired the East Country Dock Company for £40,000 and, by an Act of 1851, built another entrance from the Thames into their dock. It became known as the South Dock. Another entrance from the river was built at Lavender Lock in 1862.

Accordingly, from the four companies operating south of the river in Rotherhithe, there was now only one. The amalgamation of the Commercial Dock Company with the Grand Surrey Docks and Canal Company resulted in the formation of The Surrey

Gauge House, Greenland Dock.

The Lakes, by Shepheard, Epstein and Hunter, built on part of Norway Dock.

Commercial Docks Company. Timber was its main trade, and the company also dealt in grain. It was very profitable and regularly paid a dividend of 6 per cent. It expanded as well; Canada Dock opened in 1876, a massive grain warehouse was built, and sheds were put up to hold timber that needed to be covered. Old established businesses were demolished to make way for the new docks, such as the King and Queen Iron Works, which ceased trading in the mid-1850s. During its lifetime it made the chains that suspend the bridge over the Danube at Budapest, and those of Robert Stephenson's railway bridge over the Menai Strait.

But by the end of the nineteenth century the Surrey Docks faced competition from the newly opened Millwall Dock and the Royal Docks on the other side of the river, both of which could hold larger vessels. To counteract this pressure, the company decided to extend and enlarge the Greenland Dock. Work started in 1894 under James Maconnochie, and was continued by Sir John Wolfe Barry, who came with much prestige as the engineer who had built much of Sir Horace Jones's Tower Bridge. The project proved to be a difficult challenge for Wolfe Barry. As excavations advanced, progress was hampered by the ingress into the foundations of very fine Thanet sand. The best part of ten years was spent at a cost of £940,000 before the dock opened in 1904. It was 2,250ft in length and 450ft broad and was entered by a new lock, capable of taking the largest of ships.

The entire Surrey Docks system was now accessible from the Greenland Dock. It benefitted from its proximity to the centre of London's provisions trade in Tooley Street, otherwise known as London's Larder, and a large cold storage facility was built for cheese and dairy products. This didn't impress the London & India Dock Company, who saw their trade threatened. By way of retaliation, they offered to import timber at a 25 per cent discount. It was all of no consequence; London's docks were soon to be nationalised.

Other docks and ponds were built to the north, and by 1921 there were nine docks and six timber ponds in the whole complex. The area was largely covered in water, and land was certainly at a premium. In common with all other docks in London, the Surrey Docks came under the control of the Port of London Authority in 1909. As with their neighbours, the Surrey Docks were unable to adapt to containerisation and eventually closed in 1970. The last ship to leave was a Russian timber carrier, the *Kandalakshales*.

WHAT IS THERE TO SEE?

Most of the Surrey Docks have been filled in to make way for new housing and an ecological park, but there is still much to see.

GREENLAND DOCK. Turn right from the right-hand exit of Surrey Quays station, cross Lower Road and turn left along Redriff Road at the Surrey Docks pub (Wetherspoons). Soon on the right is a call on shelter that was formerly used for the infamous 'call on'. There is a colourful mural inside showing various aspects of dock work. Then you soon arrive at the head of the great expanse of the Greenland Dock. Walk along the left-hand side of the dock and after 400 yards, turn left at the swing bridge to see the Lakes, a novel housing development within part of Norway Dock. At the riverfront cross to the right to examine the Lock Keepers' Cabin, Tide Gauge House and Sluice, all with display boards. The entrance to the South Dock is 50 yards downstream.

LAVENDER LOCK, one of the river entrances to the Surrey Docks system, can be reached by walking upstream, keeping to the river as much as possible for about half a mile. There is a nature reserve, Lavender Pond, a little inland.

The entrance to the **GRAND SURREY CANAL** from the Thames is reached 600 yards further on from Lavender Lock. Inland from the entrance is the Grand Surrey Basin. It is beyond the scope of this book to trace the route of the Grand Surrey Canal – for those interested, see Paul Telling's *London's Lost Rivers* or **www.londonslostrivers.com**.

ST KATHARINE DOCK

In 1828, the St Katharine Dock opened close to the City, immediately downstream from the Tower of London. By this time the monopolies of the West India Dock, London Dock and East India Dock companies had expired, and the promoters of the St Katharine scheme hoped to exploit both this and the rush for free trade by building a dock with warehouse facilities as close as possible to the merchants of the City.

The site chosen covered 23 acres and on it stood the Hospital of St Katharine by the Tower, a brewery and 1,100 houses. The hospital was founded in 1148 by Queen Matilda, wife of King Stephen, in memory of two of her children who had died in infancy, 'for the maintenance of thirteen poor persons' and for prayers to be said forever for her soul. Philippa of Hainault, wife of Edward III, founded a chantry and St Katharine's became, in effect, the personal property of the Queens of England, thereby escaping the Dissolution under Henry VIII. For the dock to be built, hospital, brewery, houses and all their occupants would have to be removed. Little thought was given to the fate of the inhabitants but there was a tumult of protest at the prospect of demolishing the church. The medieval church was one of the few medieval churches to survive the Great Fire. The intrusion of the secular into the spiritual was resented (a resentment probably encouraged by the rival dock companies). 'A Clergyman' wrote of the people of St Katharine's that 'their children's children in long succession should [be able to] worship the God of their fathers, [and] that in those hallowed precincts they might lay their dust secure from indignity.' He continued, and was probably right in asserting that 'there is no more occasion for these docks than for one at the foot of Ludgate Hill'. The *Gentleman's Magazine* warned 'the destruction of this church having established a

Church of St Katharine, Royal Foundation of St Katharine.

precedent, we might have seen some future Company petitioning Parliament to appropriate the building called St Paul's Cathedral for a pawnbroker's warehouse, or some other receptacle of lumber which they might require'. And it wasn't only the building that would be missed; the church's choir was accomplished, for Stow tells us of 'the singing being not much inferior to that of St Paul's'.

Despite all protestations a Bill was duly put before Parliament in 1824 with the commendation that it would be 'expedient to make additional docks as near as may be to the City and to establish them on the principle of free competition in trade and without any exclusive privileges or immunities', the latter two phrases referring to the imminent expiry of the monopolies of the West India, London and East India Dock Companies. Much to the delight of the residents at St Katharine's, ('presenting a scene of great gaiety, the houses of every street and lane and alley were illuminated'), the Bill fell. It was presented again in another session, the leading witness being the shipowner, John Hall, who had interests at the Surrey Canal Company. The dock company based their case on the ever-increasing levels of shipping in the Port of London. They had a good case – in 1794, a total of 13,949 ships entered the port, but by 1824 this had increased to 23,618; there was similarly a vast increase in the number of vessels moored in the river.

Opening of St Katharine Dock, from an engraving by E. Duncan after a painting by W.J. Huggins.

Opposition to the plans was fierce, particularly from the London Company, who saw this near neighbour as taking away business. There was muted, if any, opposition from the West India Company. The main concern was the possibility of fire and the difficulty of getting a blazing ship out of the confined space within the dock. It was all to no avail; the Bill was given royal assent on 10 June 1825.

Everything was demolished – church, hospital and houses – and the sum of £50 was paid annually to the Curate of St Botolph's Without Aldgate for him to take responsibility for the welfare of the 12,000 souls who were displaced. Perhaps it was no bad thing, for even though Stow described the area as 'tenements and homely cottages having inhabitants, English and strangers, more in number than some city in England', the names of the streets in this crowded rookery betrayed the conditions of the people who were living there – Dark Entry, Cat's Hole, Shovel Alley and Pillory Lane.

Dock construction began in May 1827. St Katharine's Hospital transferred to Regent's Park, helped by money provided by the Dock Company, then later to Poplar; it now resides further east in Ratcliffe.[1] The capital stock of the company was £1,352,752, which was readily subscribed. The docks took two years to build and 2,500 men were employed in its construction. They are the only example in London of the work of Thomas Telford. The warehouses were by Philip Hardwick and many commodities were stored, including tea, matches, marble and even live turtles. Hardwick's warehouses were of a unique design, built flush with the edge of the water. So, rather than unloading goods from the ship to the quayside, sorting them and then redirecting them to the warehouse, Hardwick's design enabled cargo to be unloaded by wall cranes directly from ship to the warehouse floor. As it turned out, Hardwick's design worked fine if a cargo was all the same, but if it was composed of different goods, it would still have to be sorted later within the warehouse.

1   The Royal Foundation of St Katharine is now at 2 Butcher Row, E14 8DS, near the western entrance to the Limehouse Link Tunnel.

St Katharine Dock. Note the Tower of London and St Paul's in the background to the left.

The *Elizabeth* was the first vessel to enter the dock on 25 October 1828. On board was the band of the Royal Artillery who struck up 'Rule Britannia' as the vessel moved slowly into the outer basin. Interestingly, the second ship to enter was the *Mary*, a 343-ton Russian trader, loaded with eastern produce and forty veterans from the Royal Hospital at Greenwich who had fought with Nelson at Trafalgar. Telford's design consisted of an entrance basin of 1½ acres leading to an east dock and a west dock. Later, in 1856, Sir William Armstrong built a hydraulic pumping station at the dock and hydraulic power was used to operate the wall cranes. But St Katharine Dock was never really a commercial success. It proved to be too small to accommodate the new iron

FAR LEFT: Ivory housed at Ivory House, St Katharine Dock. (Courtesy of Tower Hamlets Local History Library)

LEFT: Present-day Royal Foundation of St Katharine, at 2 Butcher Row, Limehouse, E14 8DS.

ships and its lock from the Thames was only able to take vessels up to 1,000 tons. Shareholders were getting a poor financial return and in 1864 the Company amalgamated with the London Dock Company. St Katharine Dock closed in 1968 and was sold to the GLC for £1.7 million. They organised a competition for redevelopment, won by Taylor Woodrow.

St Katharine Dock now houses a marina, shops, a hotel, apartments and offices. It is also a place for relaxation: there are many boutique-like shops, several restaurants, coffee shops and a pub, the Dickens Inn.

As well as admiring the plethora of ocean-going yachts, there is plenty to see. To the left of the Dickens Inn and just before the footbridge over the entrance to the East Dock and on the quay, is Telford's Footbridge, the original footbridge that spanned the entrance to the eastern dock. It ran on rails and retracted into recesses in the dock walls. Ahead is the Ivory House, built in 1858 as the centre of London's ivory trade. It has a distinctive Italianate tower by George Aitchison, Hardwick's successor. Resistant to fire, because of its wrought iron and brick construction, it is the only

original building in the dock, and was unique at the time with its walls built directly to the water (as seen on its north side). The site of the Church of St Katharine's Hospital is at the entrance to the western dock. The site is now a branch of Starbucks, but was built originally in 1977 as a chapel to commemorate the Silver Jubilee. The coffee shop has Doric columns, salvaged from the original dock building, and on the outside, a splendid illustration of St Katharine Dock as it was when first opened.

WHAT IS THERE TO SEE?

ST KATHARINE DOCK is about 100 yards downstream from the Tower of London. It can be explored either by entering from the riverfront (just past the hotel) or from the road at East Smithfield via the splendid entrance gates with elephants each side to remind us of its trade in ivory. Nearest station is **Tower Hill**.

THE ROYAL DOCKS

By the mid-nineteenth century, steamships were rapidly replacing those of sail. Sailing ships were rarely greater than 1,500 tons and it was confidently expected that steamers would soon far exceed this value. Plans were therefore formulated for a vast new dock to accommodate these modern vessels. It was to be 1½ miles in length on the vast expanses of marshland at Plaistow, east of Bow Creek.

Plaistow takes its name from the medieval lord of the manor, Hugh de Plaiz. In the eighteenth century, smuggling and illegal prizefights were common in these lonely Thames side marshes. Gibbets and prison hulks lined the riverbank as a warning to would-be offenders. In the mid-nineteenth century, land was acquired at Plaistow by three railway contractors – Samuel Morton Peto, Edward Ladd Betts and Thomas Brassey – who formed the North Woolwich Land Company. They were joined by the mathematical genius, George Parker Bidder, also known as the 'calculating boy'. Bidder got his name from his ability, since childhood, to solve the most complicated calculations in a split second. He was paraded as part of a circus act while a youngster but in later life became a renowned engineer. The North Woolwich Land Company got the land at what was termed an 'agricultural price', and it was an astute move because in 1844 the government passed the Metropolitan Building Act to regulate the building of factories in populated areas. The aim was to keep polluting factories out of well-to-do West London and Kensington and to confine them, well out of the way, in East London. The Act was the starting gun for industrial development in lonely and depopulated Plaistow.

Three years later in 1847, the North Woolwich to Stratford railway line was built, and shortly afterwards consent was given by an Act of 1850 to build the Victoria Dock. It was the first dock in London to be built specifically to take the new, large iron steamships that were rapidly replacing the older wooden sailing vessels. The Company had capital of £4 million with powers to borrow more. The Victoria Dock was intended from the outset to link with the national railway network and was served by the Great Eastern Railway which ran along its length. The Company was also given permission to acquire 200 more acres to hold foreign cattle which it expected to import; as it turned out, the land was never used for this purpose. It was also equipped with hydraulic lifting machinery, newly introduced by Sir William Armstrong. All this gave the Victoria Dock a significant advantage over the older docks upriver. Entrance to the dock was from the west but Peto, Betts and Brassey were astute businessmen, for even while the Victoria Dock was being constructed, they bought up land to the east. It was their intention to connect the dock with the river at Gallions Reach with a canal, and so shorten the distance shipping had to travel. This land later became not a canal, but the Royal Albert Dock.

Graving Dock, Royal Victoria Dock *c.*1859.

In contrast to the older upriver docks, jetties projected perpendicularly from the main north quay, allowing goods to be offloaded from vessels alongside the jetty and transferred to waiting lighters on the other side for onward transit. The Company purchased land at the old Steelyard in the City for a warehouse to receive goods by lighter. In this way any criticism that the dock was situated too far from the city could be obviated. There were also warehouses at the dockside. Some survive, which were used as bonded stores for tobacco, near to the ExCeL exhibition centre.

The Victoria Dock was formally opened for business in 1855 by Prince Albert and paradoxically the first ship to enter was not a steamer but a 2,000-ton sailing vessel, the *Euterpe*. The dock was an immediate success, paying a dividend of 5 per cent and with confidence enough to allow ships to enter without payment of dues. In 1860, the Victoria Dock was handling 854,000 tons of shipping – double that of London Dock and a massive four times that of the ailing St Katharine Dock. This did not go unnoticed by the London and St Katharine Dock Company, which in 1864, purchased the Victoria Dock.

The original western entrance is now blocked by Silvertown Way, built to provide better road access to the Royal Docks.

It was opened in 1934 by the then Minister for Transport, Leslie Hore-Belisha, famous for giving his name to the Belisha beacon and for inaugurating the driving test for motorists.

To the east of the Victoria Dock is the Royal Albert Dock, built for the London & St Katharine Dock Company to the designs of Sir Alexander Rendel at a cost of £2.2 million. It was authorised by an Act of 1875 which passed without difficulty. The original intention was for a ship canal to give large ships access to the Victoria Dock, but then plans were changed and a completely new dock was constructed. The dock, with its entrance to the east, was intended to save journey time and to be deeper than the Victoria Dock. It is a massive 87 acres in area, 1¾ miles in length, capable of taking vessels of 12,000 gross tonnage and was opened on 24 June 1880 by the Duke of Connaught, on behalf of his mother, Queen Victoria. It was given the 'Royal' designation from the beginning, and at the same time its near neighbour was promoted to the Royal Victoria Dock. The two docks are vast in extent and in the late nineteenth century were justifiably famous as the 'hub of the Empire's trade importing every product known to man'. They specialised in chilled meat, tobacco and grain.

There was a vast cold store for imported beef and lamb. Its single-storey, red-brick Compressor House, displaying the PLA

ExCeL, Sunborn Yacht Hotel, Royal Victoria Dock.

Spillers Millennium Mills, Royal Victoria Dock.

insignia, was used as part of the refrigeration process and survives. The dock was equipped with electric lights from the start, railway tracks were on each side so that goods could be dispatched for immediate transit rather than long-term warehousing and facilities were provided for ship repair in two graving docks.

The railway ran from Fenchurch Street in the City to Gallions in the east, where the company built Gallions Hotel as an overnight resting-place for passengers on the ocean-going steamers. The North Woolwich line had to be diverted under a tunnel beneath the canal which linked the Royal Albert with the Royal Victoria. A swing bridge was also built to allow a road to cross the canal. The Company also had their own railway terminus in London at Leman Street, to the north of London Dock; it enabled goods to be transferred to warehouses there and for export cargo to be conveyed in the opposite direction.

The Royal Albert Dock was an immediate success; there were even plans to build another huge dock to the north, but these were never realised. It did, however, prompt the rival East & West India Company to set about building docks at Tilbury with, as we have seen, serious financial consequences.

Plans were formulated in 1912 for another dock to the south of the Royal Albert, linked to it and with its own entrance lock to the Thames. Work began but was curtailed by the First World War. After the war, construction began again and in 1921, the Port of London Authority opened the 64-acre King George V Dock. On 8 July 1921, King George V and Queen Mary arrived in great splendour by boat from central London, accompanied by the Duke of York and Princess Elizabeth (the late Queen Mother). As the royal party arrived, children sang a selection of patriotic songs and there were gun salutes at the Tower of London and Woolwich Arsenal. The king opened the dock to a fanfare of trumpets in the presence of the chairman of the Port of London Authority and the Archbishop of Canterbury. Tea was served in one of the transit sheds before the party finally made its way back to London. So were completed the Royal Docks. They have a total area of 245 acres and 11 miles of quay, at the time the largest area of wet docks in the world.

WHAT IS THERE TO SEE?

The Royal Docks are vast in area and best appreciated by excursions from the DLR (Beckton Branch).

ROYAL VICTORIA DOCK. Explore from Royal Victoria DLR or Custom House DLR. There are original bonded warehouses near the ExCeL exhibition centre, near Custom House DLR.

ROYAL ALBERT DOCK. Explore from Royal Albert DLR. Near to the station is the single-storey, red-brick Compressor House, displaying the PLA insignia. It was used as part of the refrigeration process for the vast cold store for imported beef and lamb.

KING GEORGE V DOCK. The latest of the three Royal docks, the King George V Dock is best seen from Woolwich Manor Way.

THE CALL ON AND THE DOCKERS' TANNER

11

Thousands of men were employed in London's docks. Before the docks were opened, men working on the river belonged to the Watermen's Company and those on the shore were members of organised brotherhoods: ticket porters, fellowship porters, tackle porters and companies' porters. Ships arriving on a tide would moor in mid-river and their goods would be transferred to riverside wharves and the Legal Quays in lighters. Depending on the cargo, they would be unloaded by one of the four brotherhoods. Ticket porters dealt with goods from America; fellowship porters unloaded cargo that could be weighed by dry measure such as salt or corn; tackle porters would weigh goods; companies' porters handled imports from specific countries. The entire process was tightly organised, and rates of pay were authorised by the City Corporation. When the docks opened, many more men sought employment. They tended to be the labourers who had dug the docks in the first place, and many of them came from Ireland. Dock work was hard, physically demanding and tedious. Broadly speaking there were two types of worker, those who loaded a ship and those who unloaded. More skilled were those who loaded. They were known as stevedores and had to load in such a way that the ship was stable in the water. Care had also to be taken to ensure the goods were placed in the right order for discharge. Less skill was needed to unload. In overall charge of a dock was the dockmaster. As well as supervising loading and unloading, he was responsible for all other aspects of the dock. It was an important position and a house went with the job. Those at St Katharine Dock and the London Dock survive.

It can hardly be said that labour relations were harmonious. The root cause of labour unrest, which was to plague the port for generations, was the system of casual labour. When the West India Dock first opened, it employed a team of 200 regular labourers, but this proved too many for regular work. The problem was the uneven flow of goods arriving at the docks. Sailing ships were ruled by the weather and an easterly wind could delay a vessel from the West Indies for weeks. Added to that, trade was seasonal – sugar and grain tended to arrive in September or April, China tea in July or November. As an example, during a four-week period in 1861, 42 vessels entered the West India Dock in the first week, 131 in the next, then 209, followed by 88 in the fourth week.

To avoid paying men to do nothing, it suited the dock companies to take on men as and when labour was required – when a ship needed to be unloaded there would be work, otherwise there would be none. This led to the notorious 'call on'. Men would assemble at the dock gate early every morning. At the 'call' they would rush forward to try to catch the eye of the dock companies' ganger who would take on as many men as were required. The system was open to obvious abuse – a pint of beer bought for the ganger in the pub the night before would smooth a man's passage.

The call on at West India Dock, nineteenth-century print.

Sometimes work was plentiful, but frequently it was not. In the leaner periods, men could be taken on for just a couple of hours' work. The spectacle is vividly described by Henry Mayhew in his *London Labour and London Poor*, published in 1851:

> He who wishes to behold one of the most extraordinary and least known scenes of this metropolis, should wend his way to the London Dock gates at half past seven in the morning. There he will see congregated within the principal entrance masses of men of all grades, looks and kinds … Presently you know, by the stream pouring through the gates and the rush towards particular spots, that the 'calling foremen' have made their appearance. Then begins the scuffling and scrambling forth of countless hands high in the air, to catch the eye of him who may give them work … All are shouting … Indeed it is a sight to sadden the most callous, to see thousands of men struggling for only one day's hire. To look into the faces of that hungry crowd is to see a sight that must be ever remembered. For weeks many have gone there, and gone through the same struggle – the same cries; and have gone away, after all, without the work they had screamed for.

Eager for work. At the call on.

Ben Tillett, dockers' leader at the turn of the century, described the scene – 'the caller on would pick and choose like throwing scraps to hungry wolves'. Later Jack Dash wrote 'the call on reminds you of a flock of seagulls converging on a morsel'.

Not surprisingly, men frequently withdrew their labour. There was a short strike in 1872, but it was nothing in comparison with the Great Strike of 1889. At the time there was very little unemployment in East London, and furthermore, the dock companies were in financial difficulty. Conditions were therefore favourable to the men. They were organised by Ben Tillett, snappy dresser, powerful orator and the founder of the 'Tea Operatives and General Labourers' Association'. His view of the men's condition was scathing: 'I cannot wonder that men lose the dignity of their manhood when they are driven helter-skelter to the gutter by a system that degrades and imbrutes.' He was later joined by fellow trade unionists and socialists, John Burns and Tom Mann.

On 7 August 1889, Tillett wrote to the management of the South West India Dock with a series of demands. He got no response and wrote again one week later. Tillett asked for an increase in pay from 5*d* to 6*d* per hour during the hours 8 a.m. to 6 p.m., and for an overtime payment of 8*d* per hour. He also appealed for the 'call on' to be restricted to two 'calls' per day to give the men a guaranteed four hours of work. (Before, men could be taken on for as little as an hour's work and then be laid off.) Finally, he also called for an end to the 'contract' and 'plus' systems.

The contract system arose when the dock companies employed contractors to take on gangs of men at the call on. The only way for men to be taken on was for them to bribe the contractors with backhanders or with beer in the pub the night before. The 'plus' system was a device used by the dock companies to discourage men from slacking and spending too long unloading a ship. It was an extra payment, paid at the end of a job at the dock companies' discretion and calculated in secret by them. This haphazard method of payment caused much resentment.

Scene from the Great Dock Strike, 1889.

By 22 August the stoppage extended over the entire port. Marches were organised each day. Tens of thousands of men would walk from the docks along Commercial Road to the employers' headquarters in Leadenhall Street. From there they would proceed to Tower Hill to hear rousing addresses from the loud and booming voice of John Burns. The rallies at Tower Hill boosted the men's confidence. Llewellyn Smith and Vaughan Nash, two East Enders who witnessed the dockers' endeavours and wrote about it, described how:

> The docker heard the plain, unvarnished truth about himself, that this strike was being fought that he might have some chance of becoming less of a brute and more of a man heretofore, that his wife and children and home might have more care.

By and large the public were sympathetic to the strikers' demands. They were swayed by the morsels of food – perhaps a crust of bread or a piece of cheese – held aloft by the men as they marched. The employers tried without success to take on blackleg labour. Money for strike pay came from many quarters – Australian dockers contributed £30,000, an enormous sum in those days. By early September there was still no sign of a breakthrough, and it was at this point that help came from an unlikely source – the Roman Catholic Archbishop of Westminster, Cardinal Manning. The archbishop – described by Tillett as 'more human, more diplomatic, more skilled in dealing with the human heart and mind than could have been found' – had the trust of the men, given that many of them were Irish Catholics. He became a member of the so-called 'Mansion House Committee', formed by the Lord Mayor, to attempt to find a way out of the deadlock. It worked well for the men. The dockers were to get the bulk of their demands, including the famous 'Dockers' Tanner', and the Great Strike of 1889 came to an end. It was to be immortalised in trade union history.

Yet, as the twentieth century got underway, the problem of casual labour remained. There was an honest attempt by the London & India Docks Committee to ease the problem with a system of four classes of dockworker. At the top came permanent workers with the benefits of sick pay, holidays and pension rights. Next came registered or 'A' workers, who were taken on by the week. Then there were preference or 'B' labourers, each designated a number and rated according to their seniority. Every night a list would be posted on the dock gate showing which men would be needed for work the next day. Finally, there were the casual men. It was intended that men should be promoted through the ranks as and when vacancies occurred.

In 1909, the PLA was founded, and two years later, seventeen trade unions combined to form the National Transport Workers' Federation. They immediately put in demands for wage increases and better conditions of employment. At first all went well, and agreement was reached with the men getting an extra $1d$ per hour, the so-called Devonport Agreement, which took its name from Lord Devonport, chairman of the PLA. The union failed, however, to sell it to the men and three days later they came out on strike. Devonport proved to be a man not to be argued with and declared that he would starve the men back to work. Ben Tillett was equally vehement in his speeches at Tower Hill, exclaiming 'Oh God, strike Lord Devonport dead'. The men eventually went back to work, but within a year they withdrew their labour again. This time the issue was their insistence that the port should only employ union members. This was the first step in the fight to make the registration of dockers compulsory – in other words a closed shop, where only registered men would be employed.

The dockers were soon to find a champion in Ernest Bevin. Fresh from successes in his native Bristol, in 1920 he spoke on behalf of the dockers at a public inquiry set up because of union demands for 16s per day, a forty-four-hour week and registration for all port workers. Bevin's advocacy proved compelling. When a professor of statistics at the University of London reported that £3 17s was sufficient for a docker to feed his family for a week, Bevin promptly purchased from a market stall the amount of food said to be enough for one dinner for a docker's family. He then returned with the meagre ingredients to the union office, cooked the food and then split the meal onto five plates – five being the average size of a docker's family. Next day the five plates were given in evidence. Bevin exclaimed, 'I ask the Court, my lord, to examine the dinner which Counsel for the Employers considers adequate to sustain the strength of a docker handling seventy-one tons of wheat a day on his back.'

Bevin won the day, the men got their raise and registration was put into effect. Men were issued with a numbered disc or tally and only men with the tally could work in the port. Thirty-seven thousand were registered at first, a number that was to fall dramatically as time went by. Later Bevin was the leading light in the founding of the Transport & General Workers' Union.

After the Second World War old problems remained, and in particular, those concerned with industrial relations. The dockers' KC, Ernest Bevin, served as Minister of Labour in Churchill's wartime cabinet. All his life Bevin had fought for the registration of dockworkers, and it was the emergencies of war that allowed him to create the National Dock Labour Corporation. Often referred to as the 'Dockers' Charter', the new body ensured that only registered men had the right to work in the docks. After the war, the newly elected Labour government set up the National Dock Labour Board to operate in a similar way. It was made up of equal numbers of employers and trade union officials, and all registered dockers were employed by this new board.

But the 'call on' remained. Men would assemble, as before, outside the dock gates. Those who got work would have each half-day's labour recorded in their registration books. At the end of the week, the men would present their registration books at the local office of the board and be paid. If no work was available, they would be required to attend the office twice every day and at the end of the week receive a fall-back payment, regardless of whether they had worked or not. If work was needed elsewhere in the port they were obliged to accept it. This in itself caused the employers difficulty, for time was always lost and ships delayed if workers needed to cross the river or come up from Tilbury. Under the new system the various port employers, such as the PLA or the numerous stevedoring companies, reimbursed the board according to the number of men they had taken on. Such were the ways of port employment throughout the 1950s.

In the early 1960s, the government set up the Rochdale Committee to look into the running of the country's ports in general. As well as other issues, the committee highlighted the running sore of casual labour, still believed to be at the root of industrial unrest. In response to their recommendations, the government appointed Lord Devlin to head a committee considering all aspects of port employment. He recommended without hesitation that the system of employing casual labour should be abolished once and for all, and on 18 July 1967, the hated system of the 'call on' was finally consigned to history. Dockers were now guaranteed regular employment for the first time since the docks opened, more than 150 years before. The PLA was charged with providing licences to those employers large enough to give jobs to men on a full-time basis.

Devlin also ended accusations of favouritism or employers using only 'blue-eyed boys', by requiring them to take on those men specified by the Dock Labour Board.

But industrial unrest remained. The equal representation of employers and union officials on the National Dock Labour Board aroused suspicion in many dockers' minds that their union was favouring the employers instead of them. In response to their fears unofficial trade union leaders emerged, and it was Jack Dash at the Royal Docks who was most prominent. Unofficial strikes became common, in particular over the question of piecework.

By the 1960s, a new container port had opened at Tilbury posing a threat to traditional ways of offloading vessels. Not surprisingly, the TGWU was insistent that new wage structures should take account of this new form of cargo handling, and promptly imposed a ban on the Tilbury container port.

The Port of London was now on the point of chaos. Both unions and employers were split. As well as their problems with Jack Dash and unofficial action, the TGWU was rivalled by the National Amalgamated Stevedores and Dockers Union (NASD). For their part, some employers favoured retention of piecework – payment by results – on the grounds that if incentives were removed, productivity would fall to unacceptable levels. Other employers saw it as the cause of all the present labour problems and a throwback to the past. They pointed to the inescapable fact that it was the machine, not the man, which was to define productivity in the new age of roll-on, roll-off ships, fork-lift trucks and, especially, containerisation. After much wrangling, Devlin Stage 2 was concluded in September 1970, and the container ban was lifted. Piecework was ended and instead men were paid a weekly wage with overtime as appropriate. Shift work was introduced as well.

But for the dockers it was a pyrrhic victory. The tragedy for them was that no sooner had the men achieved full job security and improved working conditions than the Port of London, in the upper docks at least, went into terminal decline. In 1972, the Conservative government of the day set up a committee, chaired jointly by Lord Aldington, chairman of the PLA, and Jack Jones, chairman of the Transport & General Workers' Union. Amongst other recommendations, the committee called for an improved severance scheme for the men. A voluntary scheme had existed for some years, but now many took full advantage. As a result, the number of registered dockers fell from 23,000 in 1967 to 8,800 in 1977. Very soon the number would reduce still further, and the curtain would come down on the once mighty London Docks.

WHAT IS THERE TO SEE?

DOCKMASTER'S HOUSES. The dockmaster's house at St Katharine Dock is on the east side of the entrance passage from the Thames. At London Dock, the dockmaster's house and other official houses are at Wapping Pier Head, the main entrance to London Dock. They are by Daniel Asher Alexander. Turn left from Wapping station and walk along Wapping High Street for 300 yards.

The Call On took place at the dock gates. The pillars of the dock gates to the West India Dock survive. From West India Quay DLR, walk ahead past the warehouses, turn right at the end. The pillars of the gate can be seen on the left after a few yards, next to the car park.

There is a shelter where men, waiting for the call on at Greenland Dock, would gather. Turn right from the right-hand exit of Surrey Quays station, cross Lower Road and turn left along Redriff Road at the Surrey Docks pub (Wetherspoons).

RIVERSIDE WHARVES AND THE TOOLEY STREET FIRE

In the medieval era, the north bank of the Thames within the City was lined with wharves receiving goods from all over the world. Because of theft, customs losses and smuggling due to so-called 'greedy persons', an Act was passed in the reign of Elizabeth I specifying that all goods, except for fish, were to be loaded or discharged in daylight at 'some open place, key or wharf as may be appointed by the Queen'. These wharves became known as the 'Legal Quays' and were situated along the north bank of the river between the Tower and London Bridge. Further legal quays were added by an Act of 1663 which established 'keys, wharfs or places for landing or discharging goods and prohibiting the landing and discharging of boats, lighters, ships or vessels elsewhere without the sufferance or permission of the Commission of Customs'. Goods of lesser value, such as coal, beer, stone, fish and corn, could be unloaded – as the name implies – at Sufferance Wharves, most of which lined the south bank.

When the docks opened in the early nineteenth century, the Legal Quays were badly affected. Their trade was taken away by the new dock companies who benefitted from their 21-year monopoly rights. In these circumstances, many wharves confined their business to the import and storage of corn, hemp, flax and fruit.

By the mid-nineteenth century, trade at the wharves had recovered. Three factors influenced their revitalisation. First, the monopolies enjoyed by the West India Dock, the London Dock and the East India Dock came to an end; secondly, the government was encouraging free trade, therefore duties were removed enabling riverside wharves to land goods previously restricted to the docks' bonded warehouses; thirdly, they were able to benefit from the free water clause – lighters could receive goods from ocean-going vessels within any dock and transfer them to riverside wharves, so avoiding the warehousing costs otherwise imposed by the dock companies.

Riverside wharves occupied both sides of the river, downstream to both Shadwell and Rotherhithe. Many specialised in particular goods. Fresh Wharf, near Pudding Lane in the City, imported fruit. The General Steam and Navigation Company used St Katharine and Irongate Wharves further downstream. The Royal Mail unloaded at Morocco Wharf in Wapping. Many used the latest equipment, for example, Bellamy's Wharf in Rotherhithe and Mark Brown's and Davis's Wharf in Bermondsey.

Hay's Wharf

Until the 1960s, the entire stretch of river on the south bank from London Bridge to Tower Bridge was dominated by wharves belonging to the Hay's Wharf group. Their headquarters was at St Olaf House in Tooley Street, a fine building by H.S. Goodhart-Rendell, built in 1931. To the left of the building, viewed from Tooley Street, there is a mosaic of St Olaf by Colin Gill. (It was King Olaf of Norway, who, together with King Ethelred, broke down the old wooden London Bridge in 1014 to prevent the Danes from taking London. The familiar nursery rhyme tells the story.)

Overhanging cranes unloaded New Zealand dairy products from clusters of lighters, and in the nineteenth century and before, banks of sailing ships waited in the river to unload tea from China. The area became known, with every justification, as 'London's Larder', or if not that, 'London's Breakfast Table'. In the twentieth century, 75 per cent of London's butter, cheese and canned meat was stored here!

Hay's Wharf was one of the oldest wharves on the river. It all started in 1651 when Alexander Hay took a lease on land previously occupied by a brewhouse. Hay and his sons, John and Joseph, were carpenters. They made pipes from hollowed-out elm trees that were used by Hugh Myddleton and his New River Company to convey drinking water. It was not long, however, before imported goods began to be landed at what was then known as Pipe Borer's Wharf. There were other wharves as well, such as Topping's Wharf and Pickleherring, which took its name from the pickled herrings landed from Norfolk and bound for the tables of the monks of Bermondsey Abbey. In 1793, Topping's Wharf came up for sale by auction. The sale notice described the premises in glowing terms:

The warehouses are very substantially built, in good repair, and are capable of housing 1,500 hogshead of sugar. There is space for two tiers of vessels to lie abreast next to the wharf, with a considerable and profitable trade belonging to the premises which from their situation and accommodation they will always command.

In 1838, upon the death of Francis Theodore Hay, ownership of Hay's Wharf passed to John Humphery. In 1856 Humphery asked William Cubitt to build a new wharf and at the same time construct a wet dock, Hay's Dock. In 1867, the Hay's Wharf group pioneered the use of cold storage to preserve perishable goods and in 1879 the first consignment of frozen meat was landed. The dock was used by tea clippers for unloading and that long-gone trade is evoked by the Horniman pub. The dock has been filled in and is now an underground car park. In the mid-1980s, the architectural firm of Michael Twigg Brown and Partners converted the redundant dock to shops and offices, retaining the warehouses on either side, and renamed it Hay's Galleria. Above is a fine glass and steel roof. The warehouses were built by William Cubitt at the same time as the dock, those on the west replaced after the Tooley Street Fire.

Fire was an ever-present hazard at the riverside wharves of Tooley Street. As long ago as 1696, Alexander Hay's son, Joseph, together with others, founded a mutual insurance scheme, 'Ye Amicable Contributors'. They employed six watermen to act as firefighters. The practice of insurance companies employing watermen as firefighters became common after the Great Fire in 1666. Policyholders were provided with a metal plaque to signify they were insured, and were required to attach it to the outside wall of their premises. Should a fire start, the insurance company's firefighters would arrive, and if the premises were insured, would try to put it out. But often firefighters turned up and failed to recognise their company's emblem, and would then leave and let the fire continue unabated. Such chaos led to co-operation between insurance companies and the founding, under the Scot, James Braidwood, of the London Fire Engine Establishment.

The Tooley Street Fire started in the late afternoon of Saturday 22 June 1861, and was the most devastating conflagration London had seen since the Great Fire of 1666. It began at Cotton's Wharf,

Cotton's Wharf at Hay's Wharf. Pay Day? (Courtesy of Southwark Local Studies Library)

ABOVE: St Olav's House, Hay's Wharf.

RIGHT: Tooley Street Fire Memorial.

Mark Brown's Wharf.

a warehouse containing merchandise of every sort and description. There were chests of tea and silk in the upper floors, and below were bales of cotton, hops, grain and Russian tallow. News of the fire reached the headquarters of the London firefighters – in Watling Street in the City – at about 4.50 p.m. and they were soon on the scene. An early problem was the lack of water from the mains in Tooley Street, preventing the fire from being tackled on the land.

James Braidwood soon took charge and posted his men in strategic positions, but he was unaware that some of the wharves were used as stores for government ordnance. The inevitable explosion occurred, and Braidwood and three of his men lost their lives beneath falling rubble. Other men were more fortunate and managed to throw themselves into the river. By 10 p.m. the fire was completely out of control. There were repeated explosions of stored saltpetre, as well as a torrent of liquid fire pouring into the river from the burning oil and tallow. As the crisis deepened, help was sought from floating engines in the docks and at the Tower of London. Help was immediately sent by London and St Katharine Docks, but not so from the Tower where 'the conduct of the authorities at the Tower, where there is a powerful array of engines, bore a strange contrast, for not the least assistance was tendered'.

By Sunday, all of London had heard of the disaster and thousands came to watch: 'London Bridge and all the approaches presented all the appearance of Epsom Road on Derby Day'. The fire burned throughout Sunday and by 10 p.m. 'itinerant vendors of gingerbread, fruit and coffee were carrying out a brisk trade'. The pubs took full advantage of the situation and kept their doors open late. Tooley Street was ankle-deep in melted tallow, and it was all but impossible to keep one's footing. Efforts were made by some onlookers to scrape it up and then sell it on. Thames watermen were making 2d a pound from tallow collected from the river, but some lost their lives by their rashness. Four young men in front of Hay's Wharf were scooping tallow into their boat when suddenly a flood of burning fat surrounded them. They jumped into the river in a fruitless attempt to save their lives. The fire raged for two weeks, but the newly constructed Hay's Dock (on the site of present-day Hay's Galleria) acted as a barrier and prevented it from spreading further east. As for the aftermath, £2 million of damage was done and 2,000 people were put out of work. Insurance premiums rocketed, which led eventually to the establishment of the publicly funded Metropolitan Fire Brigade.

WHAT IS THERE TO SEE?

ST OLAF HOUSE is in Tooley Street, a few yards downstream from London Bridge. The other side of the building can also be appreciated by standing on London Bridge. Further along Tooley Street a plaque on the corner of Cotton's Lane commemorates James Braidwood and those who lost their lives in the Tooley Street fire. Further on, on the corner of Hay's Lane, is a plaque to signify that here was 'London's Larder'. Hay's Galleria is a short distance away on the left. Nearest station is **London Bridge**.

Butler's Wharf

On the other side of Tower Bridge is Butler's Wharf. In its day, this was London's most extensive area of warehouses. Its early history is shadowy. John Roque's map of 1746 shows timber wharves in the area, and later there were ropeyards, granaries and shipbuilding yards. In 1794, a Mr Butler and a Mr Holland were operating in partnership as wharfingers, and then in 1872, Butler's Wharf was established as a registered public company. The manager was Henry Lafone, brother of Albert, a local politician who gave his name to nearby Lafone Street. Butler's Wharf was famous for handling tea and by 1950, 6,000 chests a day were imported. But tea was by no means its only commodity – there were rubber, canned meat and fish, rice, sugar, honey, pepper and much more.

Louise Roche has written a social and economic history of Butler's Wharf, and interviewed many dockers who gave her their own experiences of working there. Life was hard, and the wharf employed the same system of 'call on' used elsewhere in the docks. One warehouseman recalls, 'if there was a boat in a bloke called out so many and they didn't want no more'. In the early twentieth century 'they used to work all day for half a crown and sometimes they never got a day's work they only got half a day'. It was sometimes worse than that. 'They'd call them off and pay them off when they wanted to. They done two hours work, they got paid two hours money and that was it.'

Butler's Wharf eventually closed in 1972 and apart from occasional use as a setting for film and TV, including *Doctor Who*, it lay idle until restored and converted to flats by Conran Roche. What we see today from Tower Bridge is Roche's 1980s conversion of the warehouse of James Tolley and Daniel Dale. Dating from 1874, the river facade is vast. Beneath are smart restaurants, Tony and Cherie Blair entertained Bill and Hillary Clinton in one of them.

If ever a street could claim to be atmospheric, it is (or, more accurately, was) Shad Thames, the road behind Butler's Wharf. The developers are to be congratulated for not destroying it, but for those who remember it from before the late 1970s, its present form only evokes nostalgia. The restored overhead walkways remain, connecting riverside Butler's Wharf with landside warehouses, redolent of the Stygian gloom of yesteryear. It is thought that the street got its name either from the Shad fish or from a corruption of 'St John at Thames'.

The area is known as Horsleydown, from the story of poor King John falling from his horse when the animal decided to lie down (leydown) here. In Charles II's time, the riverside here was used as a place for adult baptism by total immersion. The spot was known as Dipping Alley.

Further east, there are nice converted warehouses with overhanging cranes that back onto St Saviour's Dock. The tidal inlet could well be the river outlet for the now-disappeared River Neckinger. The Neckinger flowed as far inland as Bermondsey's now long-gone St Saviour's Abbey. The monks had a tidal mill nearby and in 1536 the miller was John Curlew who, for £6 per year, was to 'grind all the corn for the use of the convent and fetch and carry the same home'.

WHAT IS THERE TO SEE?

BUTLER'S WHARF is best appreciated by viewing from Tower Bridge.

SHAD THAMES extends from Tower Bridge and then runs parallel with St Saviour's Dock.

ST SAVIOUR'S DOCK can be seen by walking along the riverfront downstream from Tower Bridge and Shad Thames. Do not follow Shad Thames to the right. It is crossed by a pleasing steel footbridge. Note the rowing boat balcony, protruding from China Wharf. Nearest station is **Tower Hill or London Bridge**.

Trinity Buoy Wharf

The River Lea enters the Thames at Bow Creek and here can be found Orchard Place and Trinity Buoy Wharf, where the curious will find many things of interest. Trinity Buoy Wharf used to be administered by Trinity House, founded in 1514 as the Guild Fraternity or Brotherhood of the Most Glorious and Undivided Trinity and of Saint Clement in the Parish of Deptford Strond. Better known as Trinity House, it has its headquarters at Tower Hill and is the official lighthouse authority for England and Wales with responsibility for providing navigational aids, such as buoys and lightships. In 1566, it was authorised to 'set up so many beacons, marks and signs for the sea whereby the dangers may be avoided and escaped and the ships the better come into their ports without peril'. In 1609, Trinity House built a lighthouse at Lowestoft and in 1803 acquired land at the end of Orchard Place where they built workshops to manufacture and maintain buoys.

There were workshops and two lighthouses, the first, which was built by James Walker, was demolished in 1920. The present one, by Sir James Douglass, dates from 1864. The lighthouses were used to train lighthouse keepers and to test the brightness of lights by observing the beam from the other side of the river at Shooter's Hill. It was to Trinity Buoy Wharf that the great scientist Michael Faraday came to do research on optics. He also assisted Trinity House by discovering ways to clear the residual gases produced by the huge lighthouse lamps which would otherwise obscure the optical equipment. Trinity House closed Trinity Buoy Wharf in 1988 and it was taken over by the LDDC. Now controlled by Urban Space Holdings, it has become a centre for the arts.

Throughout the nineteenth and well into the twentieth century there was a thriving community at Orchard Place and, with imagination, its traditional character can still be evoked today. It takes its name from a house once here called Orchard House. To the north was Goodluck Hope, land held by the East India merchant, Robert Wigram. There were five pubs – the Crown, Steam Packet, Trinity Arms, Prince Albert and the Orchard House, a school, houses and a chapel. But above all there was industry. (See *Chapter 14: Industry*.)

The toil of industry has now been given over to the arts and Container City. There is much to appreciate; Container City is represented by a mixture of businesses housed in converted ship's containers. They make a colourful and innovative change to conventional buildings. Many artists rent space in them. For example, Jem Finer and Artangel's 'Long Player' – where the sound of twenty Tibetan 'singing bowls' can be heard and repeatedly varied so that the same sequence of sound can never be heard more than once in 1,000 years! As I write it has been playing for 17 years, 286 days, 4 hours, 1 minute and 40 seconds (and a bit more now). Fourth Wall Creations have a display to celebrate the life and work of Michael Faraday and there is much more, including a couple of splendid cafés.

WHAT IS THERE TO SEE?

TRINITY BUOY WHARF and **ORCHARD PLACE** can be reached on the D3 bus from Canary Wharf or from East India DLR. Walk eastwards along Blackwall Way. Turn left at the roundabout and almost immediately at the next roundabout (Leamouth Circus) follow signs to Trinity Buoy Wharf and Orchard Place, distance about half a mile.

DECLINE AND REBIRTH

The docks were devastated by wartime bombing. Scores of warehouses, as well as swathes of port infrastructure, were destroyed. Rebuilding began as soon as hostilities ended, and in the post-war years a general mood of optimism prevailed.

By the early 1960s, it was becoming increasingly apparent that further port reform was needed. The government set up the Rochdale Committee. It made sweeping recommendations, including the observation that port expansion, in the future, was likely to be on the east coast of the country. In their conclusion – 'we think that port activity should be moved away from the centre of London' – Rochdale also raised for the first time the possible need to close London's two upriver docks, St Katharine Dock and London Dock. And they added, with much foresight, 'land at these docks could be valuable for redevelopment'.

As highlighted by Rochdale, Britain's trade was changing. Ships were increasing in size and time spent in port was money lost to their owners. Ports on mainland Europe began to rival and eventually overtake London – at the end of the war, London was handling far more cargo than Rotterdam, but by 1969 Rotterdam had not only overtaken London, but was dealing with three times as much. Shipowners began to favour the handling of cargo in bulk. The key to this shift was the introduction, soon after the war, of the humble forklift truck. Cargo of the same type could now be stacked on wooden pallets, which were removed from the ship by crane and then stacked in the warehouse with the aid of the mechanical forklift. Ominously for the men, far less labour was needed.

It did not end there. Wine was transported in bulk in purpose-built ships to specially designed tanks at London Dock and later, when London Dock closed, to a new terminal at West India Dock. Grain had been landed automatically by pneumatic tubes at Millwall Dock as long ago as 1902. Sugar, always traditionally offloaded at West India Dock by gangs of men, first in oak casks and then in jute bags, began to be unloaded by grab crane to lighters before being transferred directly to Tate & Lyle's massive refinery at Silvertown. In time, Tate & Lyle built a dedicated terminal adjacent to the refinery.

And then came the invention that was to sound the death knell for London's docks: the container system. Now cargo could be loaded into large metal containers, 8ft by 8ft by 20ft, taken by road or rail, en masse, to purpose-built vessels, offloaded at the receiving port and transported by lorry to its final destination. The impact on labour was dramatic. One giant container vessel could carry as much cargo as eight to ten conventional vessels, and be offloaded in thirty-six hours at the newly built container port at Tilbury. At the Royals, in contrast, it would take ten times as many dockers three weeks to do the job, with the dockers working ten-hour days.

There was gross over-manning. In 1967, there were 23,000 registered dockers in the port and of these 3,000 had no work each day – but by the terms of Devlin Stage 2, they still had to be paid. Newer methods of cargo handling moved on apace and trade increasingly moved, if not to Tilbury, then to Felixstowe or to the modern overseas ports. Trade in the upper docks fell like a stone. In 1971, the number of vessels in the port at any one time was 40 per cent below that of the previous year.

It was not only the docks that suffered; the same story was played out in the wharves. In 1969, Hay's Wharf in Bermondsey, for many years famous as the 'larder of London', imported its last cargo. Other wharves went the same way. The first upriver dock to close was the East India Import Dock in 1967, followed a year later by St Katharine and London Dock, and by Surrey Docks in 1970. And as docks closed, so lighterage businesses and stevedoring companies folded. The PLA found itself taking over many ailing stevedoring firms, which in the long run, only added to its financial difficulties.

Throughout the 1970s, the India & Millwall Docks and the Royal Docks remained open. Indeed, Millwall's facilities were improved, with the building of new dockside sheds and the opening of a passenger terminal for the Fred Olsen line. However, the improvements could not save the docks, and by 1980 the India & Millwall complex had closed. The Royals were in similar trouble; in 1977, tonnages were 60 per cent below the levels of 1970. By 1979 only ten berths were operational, and one year later it was just seven. The import of grain to the Royals came to an end in 1980. For a short while, the docks were used to berth laid-up shipping, but the inevitable could not long be delayed. On 26 October 1980, the Chinese ship *Xingteng* discharged her cargo, the last to be handled by the once-mighty Royal Docks.

Plans and Schemes

As the upriver docks closed, a succession of plans and schemes were laid, all aimed at deciding what to do with the newly available land. In 1971, the then Secretary of State for the Environment, Peter Walker, stepped in and together with the Greater London Council (GLC) appointed the consultants Travers Morgan 'to make an urgent study of the possibilities for comprehensive redevelopment'.

Two years later, Travers Morgan had come up with five options for the redevelopment of Docklands. Each was given a code name. *City New Town* envisaged a large proportion of new private housing with office development and a shopping centre on the Isle of Dogs. Offices were also planned for the redundant Surrey Docks. *East End Consolidated* concentrated on social housing and inexpensive private dwellings with industrial development. *Europa* planned mainly service industry and private housing centred at the Isle of Dogs, Wapping, Rotherhithe, Silvertown and Beckton. All of these centres would be linked together by a mini-tram rapid transit system. *Thames Park* favoured 700 acres of woodland, laid out as parks, together with a blend of industry and offices. Finally, *Waterside* emphasised exploiting the area's vast expanse of water by setting houses around the docks as water parks.

Travers Morgan's options were certainly imaginative and clearly set the ball rolling by concentrating minds on the future for Docklands. Unfortunately, they did not please everyone, including the Joint Docklands Action Group, an organisation of Labour Party activists and trade unionists. Many local people were alienated, feeling they had not been properly consulted. And so it was that the Conservative government of the day rejected Travers Morgan on the grounds that they 'were not prepared to set up an authority to implement development over the heads and wishes of local councils' – an interesting comment in the light of the events of eight years later.

Following the collapse of the Travers Morgan proposals, early in 1974 Geoffrey Rippon, the Secretary of State for the Environment, set up the Docklands Joint Committee (DJC) with the aim of 'preparing a strategic plan for the redevelopment of Docklands and to co-ordinate the implementation of that plan'. It comprised eight elected members drawn from the GLC and eight elected members from the Docklands boroughs. Of the borough members, there was one each from Greenwich and Lewisham and two each from Tower Hamlets, Southwark and Newham. In addition, there were eight government nominees to represent business, finance and local community interests. In 1976, they published the London Docklands Strategic Plan.

In contrast to Travers Morgan, the DJC's plan placed much greater emphasis on creating manufacturing and industrial jobs that they thought would be best suited to the skills of local people. They also wished 'to see a flourishing and viable port in East London' and an emphasis on rented council housing. It was the DJC's intention for there to be four five-year plans, spread over a twenty-year period at a cost (in 1980 prices) of £3.6 billion.

The DJC faced many difficulties. Some thought its plans to bring industry back to the area unrealistic, particularly as industry was simultaneously leaving other parts of London. Its power was limited because it owned no land and was consequently unable to allocate land or grant planning permission to prospective developers. At least 80 per cent of Docklands was in public ownership, with the PLA owning a massive 37 per cent and British Gas 12.4 per cent. The PLA's intentions for Millwall Dock and the Royal Docks were undecided, and this uncertainty was to hamper the DJC's plans. But there were some initiatives. Plans were made for Billingsgate Fish Market to move to a site at the top of the Isle of Dogs from its crowded building in the City, Cannon Workshops was to open as premises for small businesses on the Isle of Dogs and plans were made for Rupert Murdoch's News International offices to be built on the site of the filled-in London Dock. In later years, the DJC came in for much criticism for filling in docks.

Meanwhile the area was declining at an ever-increasing pace. It was estimated that 150,000 jobs were lost in the port and related industries in East London between 1967, when the East India Dock closed, and 1981. The population also fell from 55,000 in 1976 to 39,000 in 1981. Only 1,300 new housing units were built, compared with the 6,000 that were planned. Docklands had become a problem. Over 50 per cent of the land was derelict, vacant or unused.

It was against this background that Michael Heseltine, now Secretary of State for the Environment, wrote in his autobiography *Life in the Jungle*:

I had found myself in a small plane, heading in that direction by way of London's East End. My indignation at what was happening on the South Bank was as nothing compared to my reaction to the immense tracts of dereliction I now observed. The rotting docks – long since abandoned for deep-water harbours able to take modern container ships downstream – the crumbling infrastructure that had once supported their thriving industry and vast expanses of polluted land left behind by modern technology and enhanced environmentalism. The place was a tip: 6,000 acres of forgotten wasteland.

An Opportunity, not a Problem

The Conservatives returned to power in 1979. They had little or no time for the DJC, viewing it as inefficient and too slow in getting things done. So, under the terms of the Local Government, Planning and Land Act of 1980, Michael Heseltine set up Urban Development Corporations in both Docklands and Liverpool in an attempt to rectify the years of neglect that both areas had suffered. Accordingly, in July 1981, the London Docklands Urban Development Area was put under the management of the London Docklands Development Corporation (LDDC). It oversaw an area of 8½ sq. miles, stretching from the Tower of London to Beckton on the north bank of the river, and from London Bridge to Rotherhithe on the south. It was financed by government grants and by revenues generated by the sale of land.

The LDDC had far-reaching powers. It was enabled to acquire land, by compulsory purchase if necessary. Much of the Docklands, as we have seen, was in the hands of public bodies such as the PLA and British Gas, and the LDDC was granted powers over it. In contrast to the DJC, therefore, it controlled the land that was intended for development. The LDDC, controversially, took over the planning powers of the local authorities within its borders – Tower Hamlets, Southwark and Newham. In other words, it was able to grant planning permission to initiatives from private developers. It was not, however, a planning authority in its own right, nor did it control other public services such as housing, education and health, which remained with the boroughs. But it did have powers to provide and finance better infrastructure, and it was responsible for the building of new roads and the Docklands Light Railway (DLR).

LDDC's first chief executive was Reg Ward. His attitude and drive for Docklands can best be summed up by a remark he made when, after only one week in the job, he gazed over his new manor in East London from the top floor of the NatWest Tower (now Tower 42) in the City. 'What's the bloody problem?' he exclaimed. A remark that revealed – in stark contrast to what had gone before – Ward's view that Docklands was without question an opportunity, not a problem. This attitude was to characterise the entire organisation in its early years and Ward proved to be just the right man for the job, describing himself as 'a romantic dreamer, with both feet firmly in mid-air'.

The Corporation got to work immediately. The infilling of docks was stopped, and the great expanses of water began to be seen as a valuable resource rather than a mere nuisance. Home ownership was expanded, and work began on the DLR that was to link the Isle of Dogs with the centre of London. The establishment in April 1982 of an Enterprise Zone on the Isle of Dogs, in the area occupied by the West India Dock and Millwall Dock, was vital for commercial development. Developers were given tax incentives, a rate-free period for ten years, no development land tax and 100 per cent capital allowance for new commercial buildings to

be set against corporation tax and income tax. Added to this there were minimal planning restraints.

Nevertheless, there was much opposition. The root cause was the opposing philosophies of the Conservative government and the Labour-controlled local borough councils. The Conservatives viewed Docklands as a national resource to be developed in the national interest – with some public investment, but predominantly financed by the private sector. Labour, on the other hand, saw Docklands as belonging to the local people who lived there. They wanted investment directed towards housing and jobs suitable for their skills. The early years of LDDC coincided with a period when the local authorities were controlled by left-wing Labour Party activists. They saw the Corporation as totally undemocratic and instigated a policy of non-cooperation with them – effectively, the councils refused to speak to them. The result of this was that local people were denied the normal channels of communication by which to make their voices heard. It was no surprise, therefore, that local action groups were set up as a vehicle for local people to vent their frustrations and anger at what they perceived as the LDDC riding roughshod over them. Prominent on the Isle of Dogs was the Association of Island Communities (AIC).

But Docklands by the mid-1980s had become a boomtown. Massive commercial development was fuelled by the advantages conferred by the Enterprise Zone. Land and rents were much cheaper than in the City, and the 'Big Bang' Stock Exchange reforms created both a boom in financial services, and companies demanding modern computer-friendly offices. Between 1985 and 1987, the number of people working in Docklands increased from 25,000 to 42,000. Norman Tebbit, Secretary of State for Trade and Industry, spoke of 'Manhattan-on-Thames' or 'Wall Street on Water'.

And then came plans for Canary Wharf. The idea began when the US banker, Michael von Clemm, chairman of Credit Suisse First Boston, was out to lunch with LDDC executives on a floating barge, moored close to where tomatoes were landed from the Canary Islands, the aptly named Canary Wharf. Von Clemm's original scheme was for a food-packaging factory, but the food and wine must have been good, for instead, he proposed plans for a back-up office. Von Clemm flew back to New York on Concorde and put the idea to the American banker, Gooch Ware Travelstead, who was head of First Boston's property business. Travelstead had faced difficulty with proposals in the City of London and countered 'why not build a front office'. He went further and got the agreement of the LDDC and Margaret Thatcher's government for a financial services industry in the Isle of Dogs.

The scheme was sold to the Canadian-based developers, Olympia & York, owned by the Reichmann brothers. From then on everything changed; Olympia & York were quick to realise the advantages of building in the Enterprise Zone, with effectively minimal planning permission needed (Reg Ward and the LDDC were firmly on side), no public inquiry and no public discussion. They brought with them the experience gained in the development of the World Trade Center in New York. Nothing like it had been seen in London before, a massive 800ft tower, the highest building in the UK, and the centrepiece of the development, was destined to put Docklands firmly on the map.

The response of many local people, however, was far from favourable. They saw the mighty tower as more suited to the Manhattan skyline than to the close-knit and homely community they knew. Protests were immediate; 'Kill the canary and save the island' became the slogan. A barrel-load of manure was dumped outside the front entrance of the LDDC's headquarters. With some justification, a local retorted, 'they are throwing shit at us and now they can have some of it back'. Matters also got nasty when a petrol bomb was lobbed through an LDDC office window. Canary Wharf was seen as totally and completely changing the face of the Isle of Dogs. Local feeling was made plain when a procession of protesters wended its way around the Isle with a coffin carried in front 'to symbolise the death of the community'. Protests were bizarre and even comedic. At the opening ceremony of the Canary Wharf Development, the then-Governor of the Bank of England, Sir Robert Leigh Pemberton, was due to turn the first clod of soil in the presence of scores of dignitaries. Without warning, a flock of sheep was let loose from the back of a waiting lorry by a group of angry protestors. Not only that, but thousands of bumblebees were also released into the crowd. There was uproar. A marquee had been specially erected for the occasion and flowers in full bloom were set around it. The sheep spied the flowers and rushed across to eat them, knocking chairs over in the process. Apparently, Sir Robert Leigh Pemberton saw the funny side of it, but Reg Ward was less than amused, particularly when many of the visiting American bankers retired nursing bee stings. But it was all to no avail – Canary Wharf would be built.

As things worked out, Olympia & York proved to be very sympathetic to the needs and aspirations of local people. The Reichmann brothers were devout Orthodox Jews. They recruited Peter Wade, former chairman of the AIC, renowned for his part in the 'sheep-and-bees' debacle, to act as a focus for community issues. Training and education schemes were set up by the company and these coincided with a softer approach taken by the LDDC, in response to criticism it received from a parliamentary select committee. Other companies with a presence in Docklands took similar high-profile attitudes to community issues, including Barclay's Bank, British Telecom and British Gas.

The overall design of Canary Wharf was put in the hands of the Chicago firm Skidmore, Owings and Merrill. No expense was spared. Four and a half thousand were employed in 1990 with barges bringing building materials upstream from a storage facility at Tilbury. Apart from the iconic tower block (No.1 Canada Square) designed by Cesar Pelli and inspired by the clocktower at Westminster, there were six further office blocks, a shopping centre, public areas and a station for the soon-to-be-completed Docklands Light Railway.

But after a boom there is a bust. And this is what happened. Office after office was built, not only in Docklands but also in the City and Westminster. Rents fell and Olympia & York found it ever more difficult to let empty office space. Combined with the recession of the early 1990s and the costs of heavy borrowing, this

Canary Wharf (from Wapping).

working in the Docklands. In 1981, the population of the Urban Development Area was 39,000. By 1998, this had increased to 84,000. Employment in 1981 stood at 27,000. By 1998, it had risen to 85,000.

Development continued rapidly, both within the Canary Wharf complex and in the northern part of the Isle of Dogs. A series of office towers were completed in the early 2000s to partner One Canada Square, including the 200m tall and forty-two-storey HSBC Tower and Citigroup Tower. There is residential and hotel development as well. One West India Quay, a Marriott Hotel at

forced the company into receivership. Canary Wharf was then taken over by a consortium of banks, backed by Paul Reichmann, and became Canary Wharf Ltd, and later the Canary Wharf Group.

It was becoming ever more apparent that transport links had to be improved. Accordingly, the DLR was extended to Bank in 1991, to link the system to the London Underground. Another extension ran to Beckton. Further strides were made when the Jubilee Line was extended from Green Park to Stratford. The line opened in 1995 and ran directly through Canary Wharf. An underground station was built, opening a direct link between the Docklands and the mainline railway stations at London Bridge and Waterloo.

Meanwhile, as always intended, LDDC began to wind itself up. In October 1994, it withdrew from Bermondsey, and by 1998 it had ceased to exist. Its responsibilities were handed back to the local boroughs. What were its achievements? The short answer is many: 90 miles of new roads were laid out, the DLR was constructed and 24,000 new homes were built. Added to that, private sector development thrived, aided by the advantages of the Enterprise Zone, so that by 1998, 85,000 people were

Arena Tower, Millwall Dock.

its lower levels and apartments above, was built in 2004 on the quayside next to the West India Quay DLR. Skidmore, Owens and Merrill designed the two towers of Pan Peninsula, the larger with fifty floors and the smaller with forty floors of residential apartments, completed in 2009 next to South Quay DLR. The Landmark, two high-rise residential buildings, designed by Squire and Partners, was completed in 2010 at the western end of Marsh Wall. These are known as Landmark East and West. In addition, there is the Landmark Pinnacle, with seventy-five floors, one of London's tallest residential towers. Overlooking the Millwall Dock is the eye-catching forty-six-storey Arena Tower (formerly the Baltimore Tower) by Skidmore, Owens and Merrill; its twisting and sinuous design giving accommodation for 366 apartments. Completed in 2017, the tallest hotel in the UK is the Novotel Canary Wharf at 40 Marsh Wall. It has 313 rooms in the thirty-nine-storey building.

Crossrail is coming to Canary Wharf, to be renamed the Elizabeth Line. A new station has been constructed at the eastern side of the West India Quay, above which is a five-storey 'station box', 310m in length with retail and leisure facilities and a roof garden on the top. The station is due to open in December 2018 on a line between Paddington and Abbey Wood. One year later, the western end of the line will open to connect Canary Wharf with Heathrow or Reading.

Further development is underway to the east of Canary Wharf at Wood Wharf, renamed New District, for thirty buildings to include offices, residential accommodation and the iconic One Park Drive by Herzog de Meuron (architects of Tate Modern), a fifty-seven-storey apartment block in three distinct parts, named Loft, Cluster and Bay. The 23-acre New District was designed by architects, Allies and Morrison, together with architects Glenn Howells. Emphasis is placed on sustainably built residential accommodation, with plans for 3,300 new homes, 25 per cent of them affordable housing and including a new school and doctors' surgery. Newfoundland Quay is a sixty-storey residential tower by Horden Cherry Lee, to the west of Canary Wharf, due for completion in 2018. Next to the Museum of Docklands on West India Quay will be the vast Spire London, due to be built by 2020 and destined to be Europe's tallest residential tower.

And it's not only tall buildings. The East Wintergarden, designed by Cesar Pilli, is an events venue at the heart of Canary Wharf; there is opportunity for eating and drinking in a host of pubs and restaurants; for shopaholics there are 120 stores of all kinds over five malls; office workers (and anyone else for that matter) can relax at lunchtime in the Jubilee Park, a landscaped garden with serpentine water features over the Jubilee Line; there is an Everyman cinema, exhibitions, music, an ice rink open in season and the whole area is adorned with abundant public art.

Regeneration at the Royal Docks

Cargo handling at the Royal Docks ceased in 1981. The vast area stood desolate. The DJC published its London's Docklands Strategic Plan in the mid-1970s. Following the closure of the Beckton Gasworks, a programme of house building was begun. Real progress to secure regeneration didn't begin until the LDDC was formed.

First came proposals for London City Airport. In 1981, the LDDC began feasibility studies for a STOLport (short take-off and landing airport) in Docklands on the quays between the Royal Albert and King George V Docks. In 1986, Prince Charles laid the foundation stone of the terminal building and one year later the airport was officially opened by the Queen. Flights began, and grew to cover an ever-increasing number of European destinations. By 2000, passenger numbers had grown to 1.5 million per year. Expansion continued and by 2016 numbers increased to over 4.5 million per year. There are plans to extend the existing terminal and for London City Airport to get the world's first remote air traffic control centre.

Regeneration was boosted when the Docklands Light Railway was extended, first to Beckton and later to Woolwich; also by the

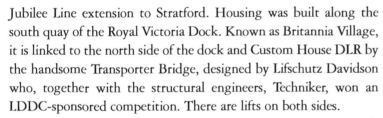

London City Airport and Tate & Lyle.

Royal Albert Dock and University of East London Residences.

Jubilee Line extension to Stratford. Housing was built along the south quay of the Royal Victoria Dock. Known as Britannia Village, it is linked to the north side of the dock and Custom House DLR by the handsome Transporter Bridge, designed by Lifschutz Davidson who, together with the structural engineers, Techniker, won an LDDC-sponsored competition. There are lifts on both sides.

In 1994, plans were laid for an exhibition centre on the north quay at Royal Victoria Dock. It was given the green light in 1998 and opened in 2000. Covering an area of about 100 acres, ExCeL (Exhibition Centre London) was built by Sir Robert McAlpine and was the largest project in Docklands since Canary Wharf. It was acquired by the Abu Dhabi National Exhibition Company in 2008. It plays host to many important trade events, including the London International Boat Show, the World Travel Market and the British International Motor Show. Many events at the 2012 Olympic and Paralympic Games were held at ExCeL – boxing, fencing, judo, taekwondo, table tennis, wrestling and weightlifting. ExCeL is London's largest exhibition centre and its coming has been followed by many hotels, including the Sunborn Yacht Hotel, berthed in the Royal Victoria Dock, outside ExCeL, the world's first luxury yacht hotel.

Thames Barrier Park, a 22-acre riverside park on the site of a former chemical works, was opened in 2000. It was designed by the French landscape architect, Alain Provost, in collaboration with the urban designers, Group Signes and Patel Taylor. It features a sunken landscaped garden and riverside promenade. The park is flanked by housing and overlooks the Thames Barrier, hence its name. The barrier, which opened in 1984, cost £500 million and protects London from flooding by surge tides.

Development at the Royal Albert Dock includes a Regatta Centre at its west end, with an international standard rowing course. At the east end of the dock is the Docklands Campus of the University of East London. The campus opened in 1999 and caters for 2,400 students. Most striking are the brightly coloured and fun, toadstool-like halls of residence. It is Teletubbies one expects to see emerging here, not students.

LDDC's responsibilities were transferred to English Partnerships in 1998 and then, in 2000, to the London Development Agency. Its first project was Building 1000 which stands on the north quay of the Royal Albert Dock. Building 1000 has aroused much controversy and was acquired by the London Borough of Newham as office space.

Emirates Airline, Royal Victoria Dock.

and prosperous they need to balance environment, economy and quality of life. These issues are explored in the Crystal's galleries.

There is a lot more going on and things to do. At the Royal Docks: the Urban Beach at the Royal Victoria Dock is a sandy beach perfect for building sandcastles or lazing in a deck chair. There are sculptures by Martin Creed, Eduardo Paolozzi, Sterling Ruby and James Balmforth, all part of The Line, a world-class sculpture trail between the O2 and the Queen Elizabeth Park. For the more adventurous, there is wakeboarding or paddleboarding available, as well as restaurants, bars and coffee houses.

And there is more to come. There are plans for housing at Pontoon Dock and Silvertown Quays. Building has already started at the Royal Albert Dock on one of the largest development projects in Europe. The area is planned to be London's third financial district catering for businesses from Asia, or those from Europe seeking to do business in the Far East. Offices, residential accommodation and retail outlets are planned by the Chinese developers ABP in a 4.7 million sq. feet scheme, the first phase of which is due for completion in 2018.

In 2010, plans were laid for a cable car across the Royal Victoria Dock from the O2 Arena at the Greenwich Peninsula. It was built by Dopplemayr, sponsored by Emirates Airline and operated by Transport for London. It opened in June 2012. The Emirates Airline Cable Car can carry up to 2,500 passengers in each direction every hour in a journey of 10 minutes, in thirty-six passenger gondolas. There is a crossing every 15 seconds and the cable car ascends to a height of 90 metres over the river – higher than the nearby O2 Arena. Fares are as per TFL: for Oyster or Travelcard users £3.50, and £1.70 for kids. Great fun!

At the west of the Royal Victoria Dock is the Siemen's Crystal, housed in an environmentally friendly building where the cities of the future are explored. The Crystal emphasises that most of us live increasingly in cities and to be successful, sustainable

The Crystal Royal Victoria Dock.

INDUSTRY

Wapping

On the corner of East Smithfield with Mansell Street is the former Royal Mint. The right of coinage has always been a royal prerogative. In 1275, William de Turnemire was appointed master-moneyer in all England, and coining was confined to the London mint. Coins were minted at this time in the Treasury and Exchequer buildings at the Palace of Westminster, but in 1300 the mint was transferred to the Tower of London. Between 1699 and 1727 the eminent scientist Sir Isaac Newton was Master of the Mint, evidently with great success:

> The ability, the industry and the strict uprightness of the great philosopher speedily produced a complete revolution throughout the department which was under his direction.

Advances in machinery and lack of space at the Tower prompted a move across the road to a new building, designed by the Surveyor to the Mint, James Johnson, and completed by his successor, Sir Robert Smirke. Opened in 1810, Johnson's Palladian building has a large central pediment with royal coat of arms and six Doric columns beneath. Coins are now minted in Llantrisant, South Wales, and minting here stopped in 1975. Behind the central facade are open-plan offices.

London Hydraulic Power Station, Wapping.

Opposite the Prospect of Whitby pub (Wapping Wall) is one of five hydraulic power stations owned by the London Hydraulic Power Company. Although patented by Joseph Bramah as far back as 1795, it was Sir William Armstrong in Newcastle who first used hydraulics to power dock machinery. Hull was the first city to have a system of hydraulic mains, but in 1883 London followed when Edward Bayzand Ellington founded the London Hydraulic Power Company. Coal-fired boilers were employed to raise steam at high pressure, which in turn drove hydraulic pumps. The pumps supplied water at an increased pressure to accumulator towers. Pressurised water was then released into a cast-iron ring main system beneath the streets, and was used for opening dock gates, powering cranes, jiggers, warehouse lifts and so on. It was Armstrong who first used accumulators to level out pressure differences between supply (the boilers) and demand (such as the lock gates). In the 1930s some 8,000 machines were powered through a network of 184 miles of mains, including the safety curtain at the London Palladium.

The Wapping station was completed in 1893. The building at the rear was the boiler house and that at the front contained the pumping engines. There were two accumulators in the tower. The company's activities declined after the Second World War, as electric power became more commonly used. The station eventually closed in 1977. It is now used as an events venue.

Another accumulator tower survives by the viaduct that carries the Docklands Light Railway (DLR), past Limehouse Basin. It is part of the old hydraulic pumping station, built in 1869 to power the lock for the new iron ships.

WHAT IS THERE TO SEE?

FORMER ROYAL MINT. From Tower Hill underground station turn sharp left, pass to the left of the remains of the medieval city wall. Cross the road (The Minories), turn right and right again, pass in front of Sceptre Court. Cross the road ahead for the former Royal Mint.

LONDON HYDRAULIC POWER STATION. Turn right from Wapping Station and right at Wapping Wall for 200 yards. On the left, opposite the Prospect of Whitby pub, is the Hydraulic Power Station.

Limehouse

Limehouse was an important industrial and shipbuilding centre. There were glasshouses, clay pipe making, sugar refining, ropemaking and bottlemaking. In 1471, the area was known as Lymeostes – a direct reference to the oasts in which lime was burnt and from which Limehouse gets its name. The first were established as long ago as 1363 by John Dick. Chalk was brought up the Thames from the downs of Kent and landed at nearby Black Ditch, a small tributary of the Thames, discernible on early maps but now just a sewer. The land was owned by the Bishop of London, who was also Lord of the Manor of Stepney. After burning, the finished product was taken to the City to be used in building. There was also a porcelain factory, owned by a Mr Wilson, which was unearthed during excavations in 1990. Examples of his delicate work, with designs showing Oriental and European subjects, can be seen in the Museum of the Potteries in Stoke-on-Trent.

Salmon and Hayre established a brewery at Limehouse. It later became Taylor Walker's Barley Mow Brewery and closed in 1960. The name lives on in the Barley Mow Estate.

Limehouse was famous for its rope works. Rope was an essential material in London's docks. It was made from manila and hemp. Rope was made by Huddart & Company. Joseph Huddart (1741–1816) was a hydrographer who surveyed coastlines and harbours. He is best known for the development of steam-driven machinery for laying up and binding rope, automating what was formerly a labour-intensive process. His rope was vastly improved in quality and reliability and set the standard for all future rope making. Ropemakers Field, a park laid out by the LDDC in Limehouse, is a reminder of the rope making industry that thrived here until the early twentieth century. There are rope mouldings on the park's railings – another nice reminder of the past.

WHAT IS THERE TO SEE?

ROPEMAKERS FIELD. From Westferry DLR walk westwards along Limehouse Causeway which soon becomes Narrow Street. The park is on the right after 300 yards. It stretches north to Limehouse Cut.

Isle of Dogs

Before the docks opened, the Isle of Dogs was a lonely and remote place. In the medieval era, land was owned by William of Pontefract. He built the small chapel of St Mary's which served a tiny community. It stood on the only road in the island that connected Poplar to the north with the river to the south. Here was the ferry to Greenwich, established as far back as the fourteenth century. It was known as Popeler Ferry and was granted to Lord Wentworth in 1550 by Edward VI. In 1626, the ferry passed to Nowell Warner, whose family were Masters of the Royal Barges. The Warners sold the ferry to the Potter's Ferry Society (a group of Greenwich watermen) for 15 guineas in 1762. Business boomed when the West India Dock opened, prompting a rival concern to set up the Poplar & Greenwich Ferry Roads Company. Rights passed to the Greenwich Ferry Company in 1888, the ferry now known as the Greenwich Vehicular Steam Ferry.

Island Gardens were laid out slightly downstream from the ferry, from which, according to Sir Christopher Wren, is 'the best view of Greenwich'; indeed, many would say the best view in London. To begin with, the view was meant not for the people who lived on the Isle of Dogs but for those in the Royal Naval College on the opposite bank. More precisely, the area was kept free from industrial development so as not to spoil the outlook for the naval officers. The park was created in 1895 as a 'little paradise for local people'. It was opened by Will Crooks, who was later the first Labour mayor in London.

As one enters the park, on the right is the entrance to the Greenwich Foot Tunnel, which replaced the earlier ferry. Will Crooks, best known for his open-air meetings outside East India Dock (later known as 'Crooks' College'), was a fervent campaigner for a free foot tunnel beneath the Thames. Many workmen from Greenwich had to make the daily trip by ferry to work in the docks and the 1d fare was a lot for them to pay. Apart from the cost savings, a tunnel would allow those living on the island easy access to the fresh air of Greenwich Park and Blackheath. Crooks succeeded, and the tunnel was built in 1902 by the LCC Engineer, Sir Alexander Binnie. Because of the experience gained with the Blackwall Tunnel, only thirty-six weeks were needed for its construction. It is about 60ft deep and there are lifts at each end. By 1905, 9,000 people were using the tunnel each week.

The west bank of the Isle of Dogs was lined with windmills; there were once at least twelve, because it was a windswept place: 'where in other parts of London the wind is scarcely felt, it sweeps over this place with great strength'. When the docks came, houses were built to cater for the increasing population and industry soon followed. The area became known as Millwall. It was described by a local clergyman in less than complimentary terms: 'badly lighted, astonishingly foul, inconceivably smelly and miserably bare and lifeless'. But the people were 'extraordinarily genial and friendly'. In 1854, the population was 5,000. There were 530 houses, 60 factories, 4 places of worship, a gasworks, post office and a station for the Thames Police.

In 1853, B.H. Cowper published a book entitled *History of Millwall, commonly called the Isle of Dogs*. He listed and described the industries that lined the banks of the Isle of Dogs, beginning at Limehouse and continuing around the entire peninsula. There were iron works, seed crushing mills, tar and turpentine distilleries, rope manufacturers, timber merchants, barge builders, wire rope manufacturers and boat builders. J.M. Blashfields, an old established firm, were on the west side of the Island. They were cement manufacturers and supplied material for Brunel's Thames Tunnel, Nelson's Column and the Houses of Parliament. They also made plaster of Paris and terracotta for the Crystal Palace.

The Canal Iron Works opened in 1809, at a site next to the western exit of the City Canal (later the South West India Dock). In 1824, Messrs. Seaward & Capel made engines at the Canal Ironworks, both for river craft and ocean vessels, including for the Royal Navy. They also fitted out warships and built swing bridges and cranes. In about 1860, the firm became Jackson & Watkins. They were taken over by the East & West India Dock Company in 1890 and ceased operating, allowing the entrance to the South West India Dock to be enlarged.

A little to the south was Morton's jam factory. It was founded by John Thomas Morton, a provisions merchant from Aberdeen, on a site previously occupied by Price's Oil Works. Morton's supplied food for the Polar expeditions of Ernest Shackleton and Robert Falcon Scott and canned food in the First World War. The football club that now plays in New Cross was founded at Morton's jam factory in 1885, as Millwall Rovers, by a group of workers of Scottish descent (hence their colours of blue and white). They lost their first game 5–0 to Leytonstone but then went on to put together a twelve-game unbeaten run. In 1910, they relocated across the river to the Den.

William Bullivant ran an iron and steel rope factory. In 1883, he was making 600 tons of rope every month. He also made telegraph wires, submarine cables, tramway cables, wire netting and aerial ropeways. In 1920, the firm was taken over by British Ropes Ltd. Their Stronghold Works received a direct hit in March 1941. Tragically, many were using the factory as an air raid shelter and forty-four lost their lives when the roof collapsed.

Levy Brothers & Knowles were sack makers. Their workers (mainly women) were forced to put up with the most dreadful conditions. They had nowhere to put their outdoor clothes, nowhere to sit down, no washing or toilet facilities. It took an Act of Parliament to improve their lot. The Sacks (Cleaning and Repairing) Welfare Order of 1927 forced the firm to provide seats, pegs for outdoor clothes, cold water washing facilities, soap and towels.

The Electrical Power Storage Company was at Sun Engine Works on the west of the island. They used lead-acid cells, pioneered by the Frenchman Camille Faure, to make batteries. The company had 300 employees and supplied temporary lighting before mains electricity was available. Their battery-powered Swan lamps illuminated the Grand Hotel in Charing Cross, the Law Courts and the Bank of England. Rudyard Kipling was a customer and had the company's lamps installed at his homes in Rottingdean and Burwash. In 1885, Queen Victoria was present at a garden party illuminated by Swan lamps at Marlborough House for her son, the Prince of Wales. In 1915, the company moved to Dagenham.

In 1852, Percival Johnson and George Matthey of the Hatton Garden assayers tried to produce silver at the British & Colonial Smelting & Reduction Company. The venture was a failure and the company was liquidated within three years. Nearby, John Wells employed 400, making corrugated iron and Stuart's Granolithic Works made artificial stone for pavements. The journal *Building News* was complimentary, writing that Stuart's had 'revolutionised footpath paving and become the paving of the world'. By 1880, they were making reinforced concrete and claimed to have used it in the construction of 1,000 buildings. All the above concerns were north of the entrance to Millwall Dock.

South of Millwall Dock was Jolliffe & Banks' Stoneyard, which won the contract to supply stonework for the new London Bridge in 1824. Massive stones were wrought into shape at the works before final dressing at the site. Next was the old established firm of Brown, Lenox & Company at Anchor Wharf. Before moving to Anchor Wharf the firm made chains in Narrow Street, Limehouse. It was founded by Samuel Brown, who patented the stud link chain that replaced hemp ropes. The company supplied chains for the Royal Navy from 1810 until the First World War, including for the *Great Eastern* and the *Mauretania*. They also made buoys, water tanks, coal bunkers, chimneys and gantries. They were eventually taken over by the F.H. Lloyd group and finally closed in 1980.

Following on was the Millwall Iron Works of John Scott Russell (see *Chapter 15: Shipbuilding*), much of which can be appreciated at Burrells Wharf. Burrells were oil refiners, manufacturers of paints, varnish and colours. They were established in the Minories, near to the Tower of London, in 1852 and moved to buildings previously occupied by the Millwall Iron Works which they extended. Burrells was incorporated in 1912 and became a public company in 1947. Much remains of the Millwall Iron Works including a chimney and the Plate House built for Scott Russell by William Cubitt.

Continuing around the island, there was a disinfecting fluid manufacturer, more chemical works, a pottery and the ferry to Greenwich. The east of the Isle of Dogs was developed later than the western side. The next mile of riverfront is taken up by Cubitt Town, taking its name from William Cubitt who developed the area in the mid-nineteenth century. Born in Norfolk, he was the brother of Thomas Cubitt, another eminent builder. In 1843 he began development, having leased a large area of land to the east of the Isle of Dogs from the Countess of Glengall. As well as houses, he built a series of wharves and manufactories along the bank of the river. There were cement factories, potteries and timber wharves. All have now gone, many destroyed by wartime bombing and now replaced by housing. There were pubs as well, including The City Arms, Anchor and Hope, Torrington Arms, Tooke Arms, King's Arms, Glengall Arms, Robert Burns, Ferry House, Newcastle Arms and the Folly House.

Early morning is the best time to view the action at Billingsgate Market, and this means between 4.30 a.m. and 8.30 a.m. (sorry). The converted transit shed, at the head of the Isle of Dogs, is the successor to the famous Billingsgate Fish Market in Thames Street in the City. The name probably derives from a Saxon man, Beling, who was a local landowner. In 1327, Edward III granted

ABOVE LEFT: Burrells Wharf.

LEFT: John Scott Russell's Premises, Millwall Iron Works.

Millwall Dock Central Granary.

Billingsgate a charter that prevented rival markets setting up within 6.6 miles. (This was the distance that, within one day, a man could reasonably walk to Billingsgate, sell his goods, and then return home.) In those early days Billingsgate traded in all sorts of commodities, including coal, corn, iron, pottery, salt, wine and fish and it was not until about 1699 that the market was restricted solely to the fish trade. It was particularly notorious for the bad language of its porters, who wore special hats based on those worn by the longbowmen at the Battle of Agincourt. Sir Horace Jones's fine building in Thames Street was converted by Richard Rogers for the financial services industry in 1982, and the fish market moved to its present site on the Isle of Dogs. The original Billingsgate Bell survives at the new market and there is a copy of the clock from the old market hall. The market is managed by the Corporation of London and early every weekday morning lorryloads of fish arrive from all points of the globe. The new building has a large floor space and the method of trading follows a well-established set pattern. Samples of fish are brought to the market hall by licensed porters and put on display. This is known as 'shoring in'. Buyers place their orders and porters collect the sales orders from the suppliers and 'barrow' them to the buyers' vehicles. For this service, the buyer pays the porter 'bobbin money'. Every year, as rental payment, a gift of fish is given to the Mayor of Tower Hamlets who then distributes it to the residents of old people's homes.

McDougall's started in Manchester in 1846 when Alexander McDougall opened a chemical works. He soon discovered a new baking powder and in 1869 his sons set up a fertilizer plant on the south quay of Millwall Dock. In 1879, McDougall's self-raising flour was born, soon to become a household name. The plant suffered a disastrous fire in 1899 when, despite the attentions of twenty-five fire engines from all over London, the original mill burnt down. It was replaced by the Wheatsheaf Mills a couple of years later. In 1935, enormous concrete silos were erected and became a familiar landmark. The company was later to become part of Rank Hovis McDougall. The Millwall Granary closed in 1982.

Hooper's Telegraph Works were founded by William Hooper in Mitcham. He dealt in rubber goods, mainly for the medical profession, before diversifying to electrical insulation cables. Hooper's moved to Millwall Dock on the Isle of Dogs in 1870 and manufactured and lay submarine communication cables. Their first contract was for the 2,300-mile cable linking Vladivostok with Hong Kong.

WHAT IS THERE TO SEE?

MILLWALL IRON WORKS AND BURRELL'S WHARF. From Island Gardens DLR, turn right for about 400 yards. John Scott Russell's premises are clearly seen on the left, just past the Ship pub. Next is Burrells Wharf.

BILLINGSGATE MARKET. Leave the eastern exit of Canary Wharf Jubilee Line Station, walk ahead to Montgomery Square, turn left into Montgomery Street and at the crossroads, turn right over the bridge and exit the Canary Wharf estate by the vehicular exit, Trafalgar Way. On the left is Billingsgate Market.

Bow Creek (Leamouth)

The River Lea rises near Luton, and it is said the Romans used it to reach their important city of Verulamium (St Albans) from the Thames. In 896, King Alfred the Great, together with a fleet of his ships, is said to have pursued the Danes along it. The area has been heavily industrialised since the mid-nineteenth century and its pollution was summed up in *Punch* in 1885 with a poem called 'The Rowers on the Lea':

Within a brief half hour,
They sang but not in glee,
We envy folk upon the bank,
but they don't envy we!
For why? We feel inclined to faint,
We're sick as sick can be;
We've all got germs of typhoid from
This rowing on the Lea.

As well as this there was:

There are ten bad smells of Lea,
They are vile as vile can be
And there they are, and there they'll be,
Unless to the matter the public see,
Those ten bad smells of Lea.

The plight of the River Lea was a direct consequence of the Metropolitan Building Act of 1844, which sought to protect populated areas (in practice the well-to-do West End of London) from the new, noxious-smelling industries of the nineteenth century. The River Lea doubles back on itself in a U-turn before entering the Thames at Leamouth or Bow Creek. The first industry to come to Leamouth was a copperas works on the river's west bank. Copperas is ferrous sulphate, which is used in the dyeing industry. John Strype mentioned in 1720, 'a large works wherein a great quantity of copperas is made every year'. In 1787, the concern was taken over by John Perry, of Blackwall Yard.

The northern end of the peninsula, known as Goodluck Hope, was taken up by the Thames Plate Glass Works. They were here from 1835 until 1874, the only company making plate glass in the south of England and one of only six in the country. Their plate glass was used in the manufacture of mirrors and later shop windows. They employed many women because of the light touch and dexterity needed for grinding and polishing. In 1862, John Pepper was employed at the works. He was successful in producing a plate glass that was designed to give an optical illusion on a stage whereby people seemed to disappear! The Plate Glass Company closed in 1874 and was succeeded by the Thames Bag and Sack Company, which suffered two serious fires in 1912 and 1935. James Mather, a city merchant, opened at Orchard Place in 1780. He boiled and processed the whale blubber landed at Greenland Dock. It was a noxious process and certainly one of the ten bad smells of Lea referred to in the poem. Boiling was necessary to extract the whale oil which was used in the manufacture of soap and for lighting. The shell of Mather's building still stands. The renowned Scottish shipowner, Donald Currie, had his Castle Main Packet Company here and ran ships to Cape Town. He merged with his principal competitor, the Union Steamship Company in 1900 to become the Union Castle Steamship Company, and in 1932 the Union Castle Line, finally leaving Orchard Place in 1956. Also at Orchard Place were Ditchburn & Mare, the Thames Iron Works and Samuda Brothers.

WHAT IS THERE TO SEE?

The derelict premises of **JAMES MATHER, DITCHBURN AND MARE**, the **THAMES IRON WORKS** and **SAMUDA BROTHERS** can be seen in Orchard Place. Take the D3 bus from Canary Wharf or alternatively, from East India DLR walk eastwards along Blackwall Way. Turn left at the roundabout and almost immediately at the next roundabout (Leamouth Circus) follow signs to Trinity Buoy Wharf and Orchard Place, distance about half a mile.

Silvertown

In 1846, a railway line was laid between Stratford and North Woolwich by the same promoters who later built the Victoria Dock. It quickly spurred industrial development. First to take advantage was Charlie Mare, a landowner from Cheshire, who was a partner in the iron works of Ditchburn and Mare, which relocated from Deptford to Orchard Yard on the west side of Bow Creek in 1836. The firm imported its iron from the north, but to save money, Mare suggested they buy land on the Essex side of the creek and roll their own. Ditchburn wouldn't go along with the idea and so the pair broke up and Mare started up on his own, buying 4 acres of land. As well as ships he built the Menai Tubular Bridge and the new Westminster Bridge. Mare got into financial difficulty when he tendered too low for a contract to supply gunboats for the Crimean War and his works were taken over by the Thames Ironworks & Shipbuilding Company (see *Chapter 15: Shipbuilding*). He surfaced again at the Millwall Iron & Shipbuilding Works, married a 'great beauty', became MP for Plymouth, was friendly with Benjamin Disraeli, but died in poverty in Limehouse.

Aerial view Silvertown Rubber Works. (Courtesy of Newham Local Studies Library)

The next firm to open between Bow and Barking Creek was a glass factory owned by the Howard brothers. Big changes came to the area when the Victoria Dock opened; the railway was also extended north of the dock and William Cory opened a coaling station. This had the effect of reducing the price of sea coal, enabling the Thames side factories to compete with those in the north.

The area was first called Hallsville, but then came Stephen Winckworth Silver, who gave Silvertown its name. Silver started out in Greenwich in the early nineteenth century, making waterproof clothing, belting for machinery, ebonite and general rubber goods. In 1852, Silver moved across the river to just west of North Woolwich and in 1864 launched the India Rubber, Gutta Percha & Telegraph Co. Charles Hancock (formerly of the West Ham Gutta Percha Co.) joined him and they set about making and laying cables. Copper wire was used as the conducting medium. First it was wound onto bobbins and then several lengths twisted into a wire rope which was insulated with gutta percha. The cable was coated with jute and was further protected by windings of iron wire. The company got an early order from the Western Union Telegraph Co. of the USA for a cable from Florida to Havana. By the 1870s it had purchased two cable-laying ships, the *Dacia* and SS *International* and had laid a cable from the Channel Islands to the English coast. They bought the first custom made cable ship, the *Hooper*, from Messrs. Hooper of Millwall Dock and renamed her the *Silvertown*. By the beginning of the twentieth century the firm was making bicycle and motor car tyres and by 1923 employed 4,000 workers on its 17-acre riverside site. The factory, now acquired by the British Tyre and Rubber Co., was badly bombed in the Second World War. In 1955 it was renamed the Silvertown Rubber Co. Rubber production ceased in Silvertown in the 1960s.

Henley's, the firm founded by William Thomas Henley, were leaders in cable manufacture. Henley was born in 1814 in Midhurst, son of a fell monger and glover. He arrived in London as a young man of 16 and worked as a labourer for a silk merchant in Cheapside before becoming a docker at the newly opened

Aftermath of Silvertown Explosion. (Courtesy of Newham Local Studies Library)

St Katharine Dock. But science and technology was his abiding interest, in particular electromagnetism. Henley set up on his own in Whitechapel making electrical equipment and eventually settled at Enderby's Wharf in East Greenwich.

Henley's specialised in the manufacture of long lengths of telegraph cable. They linked Manchester with London, and Liverpool and Dublin with Belfast. The firm later expanded to make submarine cables and built new riverside works at North Woolwich. William Henley can be thought of as a founder of the modern communications industry. He died in 1882. The firm he founded also made house wiring, telephone cables, power cables for the electricity supply industry and much more. In 1959, Henley's were acquired by AEI, then GEC and are now part of TT Electronics.

By the early twentieth century there were twenty large firms in Silvertown. They included Odam's Chemical Manure Works that used the blood of freshly slaughtered cattle from their own abattoir to make fertilizer – the stench must have been dreadful! In 1896, the Mineral Oils Corporation (Minoco) was formed when Charles Hunting began to distil and refine lubricants from Russian crude oil imported by the parent company, the Northern Petroleum Tank and Steamship Company of Newcastle upon Tyne. Five years later the company was known as Silvertown Lubricants and from a 13-acre site supplied oil to railway companies. In 1929, it was taken over by Gulf Oil. By the 1960s distilling had given way to oil blending.

The chemical works of Brunner Mond were at Crescent Wharf in Silvertown. There were two plants, one making soda crystals from ammonia and the other caustic soda. In the Great War they were asked to convert their plant to purify TNT as part of the war effort. Brunner Mond were unwilling at first, and well they might have been, for within 400 yards of the works were 3,000 residents, a school and a church. However, they eventually agreed to the government's demands and production started. The process consisted of dissolving 5-ton batches of TNT in a melt pot with alcohol, then crystallising and packing into 50lb cotton bags. On Friday, 19 January 1917, a fire started in the melt pot room resulting in the largest ever explosion experienced in London. The appalling Silvertown Explosion killed 73 people and 2,000 were made homeless. The blast, as 50 tons of TNT exploded, was heard as far away as the south coast. The cause of the explosion was never determined – some said it was sabotage, but poor safety procedures were more likely. The explosion was a disaster waiting to happen. Chief scientist, F.A. Freeth, wrote that 'it was manifestly very dangerous. At the end of every month we used to write to Silvertown to say that their plant would go up sooner or later, but were told it was worth the risk.'

Edward Cook was a soap manufacturer in Norwich. In the 1830s, his firm moved to Goodman's Yard in Whitechapel, and then in 1859 to Cook's Road in Bow on the banks of the River Lea in a factory known as the 'Soapery'. Edward Cook's son (also Edward) was a distinguished chemist and for a time Member of Parliament for West Ham. Many women worked in the soap-packing department; the most popular brand being

John Knight Royal Primrose Soap Works. (Courtesy of Newham Local Studies Library)

'Throne Toilet Soap' said to have a fragrance like 'a Devonshire cottage garden on a lovely May morning'. After the Second World War, Cooks were taken over by Knights. Knight's Castile soap was introduced in 1919 by John Knight Ltd. The original 'Castile' soap was made in Castile, Spain, from olive oil and soda. First at Wapping, they moved to Silvertown at the Royal Primrose Soap Works and are now part of Unilever. In 1919, the firm employed 1,200 people.

James Keiller made marmalade in Silvertown. He arrived in the area from Scotland in 1880 and built a large factory in Tay Wharf. The firm was later taken over by Crosse and Blackwell, and then in 1969 by Nestlé.

There were three large mills beside the Royal Victoria Dock. One, built by the Co-Operative Wholesale Society, occupied 5 acres. Premier Mill, of Joseph Rank Ltd was nearby. It became Rank Hovis McDougall. There was also Millennium Mill by W. Vernon and Sons. It was destroyed in the Silvertown explosion and rebuilt as Spillers.

Flour Mill, Royal Victoria Dock.

ABOVE: Tate & Lyle, Silvertown.

LEFT: Henry Tate & Son, 1890s. (Courtesy of Newham Local Studies Library)

Silvertown is, above all, known for the sugar industry. It all began with Henry Tate, son of a clergyman, who was born in Lancashire in 1819. He set up on his own as a grocer and in 1859 went into partnership with John Wright, a sugar refiner of Liverpool. But the call of London was strong and in the mid-1870s Henry Tate bought land in Silvertown, previously occupied by a shipyard, and built a sugar refinery there. But the poet, Tony Tate, tells the story better:

> Then he called seven sons into office
> And said 'Four up here will remain.
> But Edwin and two go to London'.
> Ted said 'Is the man really sane?
> 'He's bought up a marsh and a gasworks
> At least seven miles out of town.
> We'll either go down with swamp fever
> Or whole ruddy workforce will drown.'

To replace the somewhat inconvenient procedure of producing sugar loaves, Henry Tate was quick to exploit a German patent that enabled sugar to be produced in cube form and it was at Silvertown that Tate made his famous sugar 'cube'. Henry Tate is remembered for his collection of paintings and bequest of money, which made possible the famous Tate Gallery:

> Sir Henry Tate, Bart
> Was a lover of art
> Whom the nation should thank
> For his gallery on Millbank

Abram Lyle was a Scot who started his working life in a lawyer's office. He later joined his father's cooperage business, then entered shipping, and was involved, amongst other things, in transporting sugar. This led to his interest in sugar refining and in particular golden syrup:

> So that was the start of his venture
> Which prospered and famously grew
> On sugar and Lyle's Golden Syrup
> (Which Tate's call 'that Devil's Brew').

In 1881, Abram Lyle bought land just over a mile upstream of Tate's refinery near Odam's and Plaistow Wharf, and started to make Golden Syrup. Henry Tate & Sons and Abram Lyle & Sons amalgamated in 1921 after the deaths of the founders. The firm's trademark is taken from Judges, Chapter IV – the lion that Samson killed full of honey and surrounded by bees, hence the solution to Samson's riddle 'out of the strong came forth sweetness'.

Raw sugar arrives at the Silvertown refinery in specially equipped sea-going vessels as moist brown sugar coated with molasses. The first refining process is affination. Warm syrup is added to soften the molasses and the mixture, known as magma, is centrifuged to separate off the syrup. At the carbonation stage the sugar crystals are dissolved in water, lime added, and carbon dioxide bubbled through to form chalk, which traps the impurities which are then filtered off. The resulting liquid is passed over charcoal to remove colour and is then boiled in vacuum pans to induce crystallisation. After centrifuging, a damp sugar results which is dried in large revolving cylinders in a stream of hot air.

WHAT IS THERE TO SEE?

SPILLERS MILLENNIUM MILL. The derelict mill can be seen on the south side of the Royal Victoria Dock.

TATE AND LYLE SUGAR REFINERY. Can be seen from the Woolwich branch of the DLR.

Bermondsey

The former Courage Brewery is situated just downstream of Tower Bridge.

The Revocation of the Edict of Nantes in 1683 exacerbated the persecution of Protestants, already rife in France. Many sought refuge in Britain, among them the Courage family who settled in Aberdeen. In 1780, John Courage, son of Archibald, arrived in London as agent for the Glasgow based Carron Ships. It was not long before he paid John and Hagger Ellis £616 13*s* 11*d* for their riverside brewhouse in Horselydown, Bermondsey. Disaster struck at the brewery in 1891 when a spark in the malt house caused an explosion and fire. For the next few weeks until the brewery was rebuilt, Courage's had to take beer from their nearby rival, Barclay Perkins (and pay them £40,000 for it). In common with other large brewers, Courage's absorbed smaller concerns in the early twentieth century. In 1955, they merged with their neighbours, Barclay Perkins, took over Simmonds of Reading in1960 and John Smith of Tadcaster in 1970. They were acquired by the Imperial Tobacco Group in 1972. Brewing stopped at Bermondsey in 1982.

Biscuit manufacture is a distinctly British institution, mainly due to the climate being particularly suitable for producing ideal wheat flour. Peek Frean of Mill Street, Bermondsey, began when Mr Peek, a tea merchant in the City, invited George Hender Frean, a miller and ships' biscuit maker from the West Country, to manage a biscuit factory he had set up for his two sons. As it happened, his sons had little or no interest, but Peek Frean nevertheless went from strength to strength. In 1865 they introduced their 'Pearl' biscuit, the pioneer of the modern biscuit – crisp, crumbly and very palatable. They swept the country, and moreover played a momentous part in feeding the starving

The Former Courage Brewery, Shad Thames.

of Paris after the Franco-Prussian War – the French government buying 16,000 tons of Peek Frean's best biscuits in 1876 to relieve the siege of Paris. By this time fire had ravaged the Mill Street premises and the firm expanded to Drummond Road to the south-east. Henry Mayhew, the well-known social researcher of London life, paid a visit and paints a pleasant picture:

> There was a lovely smell of the sweetest flow pervading the immense room which was filled with the haze of the powdery white particles, till the atmosphere seemed to be as gauzy as a summer morning mist. The bakery itself was about as long as between the decks of an Indianman, but as lofty as a railway terminus and heaven knows how many of these same biscuits making machines were at work at the same time.

In 1921, Peek Freans amalgamated with Huntley and Palmers and formed Associated Biscuit Manufacturers. Then in 1969 they joined with Jacobs to become Associated Biscuits Ltd. In 1982, they became part of the American multinational Nabisco. Manufacture ceased in Bermondsey in 1989. Also in Mill Street were Spillers Pet Foods and Vogans who imported oats, lentils and peas into the adjacent St Saviour's Dock.

Beckton Gas Works. (Courtesy of Newham Local Studies Library)

WHAT IS THERE TO SEE?

THE FORMER COURAGE BREWERY. Can be seen from Tower Bridge and from Shad Thames.

PEEK FREANS, **SPILLERS** and **VOGAN'S** were in Mill Street, which can be reached by walking along the riverfront downstream from Tower Bridge and Shad Thames. Do not follow Shad Thames to the right. Cross the pleasing steel footbridge. Note the rowing boat balcony, protruding from China Wharf, and enter Mill Street.

Beckton

In 1807, at the Crown and Anchor Tavern in The Strand, the first meeting of the New Patriotic Imperial and National Light and Heat Company was held. It was not long before this became the Gas Light and Coke Company (GLCC). Then in 1812 it was granted a Royal Charter by the Prince Regent, on behalf of George III, giving the company power to raise capital with limited liability, to dig up streets and lay mains to supply gas to the City, Westminster and Southwark. The company, by virtue of being established both by Royal Charter and Act of Parliament, had a governor and a court, rather than a chairman and board of directors.

The company's first works were at Canon Row, Westminster, a stone's throw from the Palace of Westminster and their offices were at 96 Pall Mall. The company was full of ambition with plans to light the approaches to Parliament to gain maximum publicity. They overstretched themselves and failed to deliver, but the day was saved by the appointment of Samuel Clegg who was paid at a salary of £500 per year. (It was said of Clegg 100 years later that 'perhaps there is not another individual to whose zeal and

Retorts at Beckton Gas Works.
(Courtesy of Newham Local
Studies Library)

ability the art of gas making is so much indebted for the variety as well as extensive utility of his inventions and improvements'.) He realised at once that the Cannon Street works were entirely inadequate. The outcome was a move to a much larger site at Providence Court, Great Peter Street (at the junction of Great Peter Street and the present-day Horseferry Road). So was born the Westminster Gasworks, the first permanent gasworks for public supply in the country.

In the years that followed many companies consolidated and merged and of these the Gas Light and Coke Company dominated. In 1848, they appointed Samuel Adams Beck to their board; in 1852 he became deputy governor and in 1860 governor. It was Beck who, on 19 November 1868, drove the first pile into the river wall at Gallions Reach, near Barking. On the following day the Court of the GLCC resolved that the company's new property and works at Barking Creek should henceforth be known as Beckton after their governor. The Beckton works covered some 627 acres and became the largest gasworks in the world. Today, although the works are long gone, the area is still known as Beckton.

SHIPBUILDING

It is perhaps difficult for us to appreciate today that until the late nineteenth century a flourishing shipbuilding industry thrived on the banks of the River Thames. In the medieval era it was supervised by the Worshipful Company of Shipwrights, who regulated work practices and imposed strict standards of workmanship. Edward III, in his assault on Calais in the Hundred Years War, had twenty-five ships built on the Thames, a number exceeded only by those from Dartmouth. The shipbuilding yards thrived in the nineteenth century, but with the advent of iron ships, bringing both coal and iron to London proved too expensive and so by the end of the century most firms moved to the north or closed. Those remaining concentrated on ship repair.

Limehouse

There was shipbuilding in Limehouse (or Ratcliffe as it was then known) in the fourteenth century; its vessels fought in the Hundred Years War. There is much to see in Narrow Street: Dunbar Wharf belonged to Duncan Dunbar, a wealthy Limehouse-born shipping magnate. Dunbar had a large fleet of ships, which carried passengers and cargo to the Far East and Australia. They carried everything, from deported convicts to beer from the nearby Barley Mow Brewery.

Shipbuilding at Limehouse, the *President* on the stocks. Note St Anne's Limehouse in background. (W. Parrott, 1840)

John and Robert Batson, in 1751, inherited a yard just downstream of Limekiln Dock. It was previously owned by their uncle, Robert Carter, described as a 'shipbuilder of the hamlet of Poplar'. Batson's built seventeen ships for the Royal Navy, including HMS *Phoenix*, captained by the Duke of York – the brother of King George IV – and HMS *Captain*, Nelson's ship at the Battle of St Vincent. Nelson later commanded *Janus*, another of Batson's ships, in 1780. She was described as a 'fine frigate, quite new'. In 1800, Batson's Yard was transferred to Curling,

Young & Company which built East and West Indiamen, all of timber, also the *President*, at the time the largest paddle steamer in the world. Their yard became known as Limehouse Dock Yard. The Royal National Lifeboat Institute (RNLI) bought lifeboats from Harton of Limehouse and Forrests. J. & A. Blyth was also at Limehouse and was associated with the sugar planters in the West Indies. They eventually closed in 1876.

WHAT IS THERE TO SEE?

DUNBAR WHARF is in Narrow Street. From Westferry DLR walk westwards along Limehouse Causeway soon becoming Narrow Street. Dunbar Wharf is about 250 yards on the right.

Isle of Dogs

Millwall Iron Works and the Great Eastern

It all started with William Fairbairne, a Scottish-born engineer and shipbuilder. He was a colleague of both Robert and George Stephenson and advised Robert on the design of the Britannia Bridge across the Menai Strait. His main yard was in Manchester but in 1835 he came to Millwall and began to build iron ships, including many for the Admiralty. In the adjacent yard another Scot, David Napier, was also building iron ships to innovative designs. In 1853, his yard was devastated by fire. Before long, yet another Scot arrived. He was John Scott Russell, a graduate of the University of Glasgow and former Professor of Natural Sciences at Edinburgh University. Having acquired the Millwall shipyard in 1848, and in partnership with Isambard Kingdom Brunel, he set about building the *Great Eastern* for the Eastern Steam Navigation Company. Both were experienced men. Scott Russell's academic background enabled him to apply innovative scientific principles to the steamships he designed at Caird's Greenock Shipyard in Glasgow. Brunel had designed ships before, including the wooden ocean-going *Great Western* and the *Great Britain*, the first iron vessel to cross the Atlantic.

The Eastern Steam Navigation Company sought to exploit the growing trade with Australia but was hampered by having to maintain a string of coaling stations for its ships to refuel en route. The solution was the *Great Eastern*, which was designed to hold enough coal for the entire round trip, as well as room for plenty of passengers and cargo.

The ship's specification was impressive. She was 211m in length, 37m wide, had a displacement of 22,500 tons and could steam at 14 knots. She could carry 12,000 tons of coal with 800 first-class and 3,000 second-class passengers, or alternatively there was room for 10,000 troops. It was a massive project, estimated by Scott Russell at £500,000. In the event – Scott Russell proving to be far a better engineer than businessman – costs overran, and Scott Russell went bankrupt. Brunel, furious at what had happened, took over full control and construction began again.

Great Eastern Slipway, Isle of Dogs.

By November 1857, the great ship was ready, its vast dimensions necessitating a sideways launch into the Thames. The date was set for 3 November 1857 and well over 100,000 people gathered, both in Millwall and across the Thames at Deptford, to witness the sight. They came from all sections of society; there were beggars, bankers, dignitaries of the church, old women and young men – but all were to be disappointed! Isambard Kingdom Brunel had devised a complicated system of hydraulic rams, chains and brakes to launch his ship, but she stubbornly refused to move. One man was killed in the process and others walked off the job. Charles Dickens was one of the spectators and he wrote:

A general spirit of reckless daring seems to animate the majority of the visitors. They delight in insecure platforms; they crowd on small, frail housetops; they come up in little cockleboats, almost under the bows of the great ship. In the yard, they take up positions where the sudden snapping of a chain, or the flying out of a few heavy rivets, would be fraught with consequences that they have either not dreamed of, or have made up their minds to brave. Many on that dense floating mass on the river and the opposite shore would not be sorry to experience the excitement of a great disaster, even at the imminent risk of their own lives. Others trust with wonderful faith to the prudence and wisdom of the presiding engineer, although they know that the sudden unchecked falling over or rushing down of such a mass into the water would, in all probability, swamp every boat upon the river in its immediate neighbourhood, and wash away the people on the opposite shore.

There followed a series of attempts to get the great ship into the river, all to no avail. In the end, Brunel called in Robert Stephenson for advice and the Birmingham firm of Richard Tangye was engaged to provide rams to provide much more force. It worked, both for Brunel and the fortunes of Tangye's company, Tangye remarking 'We launched the *Great Eastern* and the *Great Eastern* launched us'. Launching alone cost £172,000, but all seemed set fair in January 1858, with the bells of the Church of St Nicholas, Deptford, ringing in the background, as the *Great Eastern* eventually slipped into the River Thames. All that remained was for the public rooms to be fitted out. No expense was spared, the contract going to Crace and Son of Wigmore Street, better known for their work for Augustus Welby Pugin at the new Palace of Westminster.

Regrettably the *Great Eastern*, which cost £920,000 to build, was not a financial success. There followed one catastrophe after another. No sooner had she left the Thames, in preparation for her maiden voyage, than an engine failure caused a boiler to explode, resulting in six fatalities, *The Times* reporting: 'the fore part of Mr Crace's beautiful saloon became a pile of glittering rubbish'. The *Great Eastern* did eventually cross the Atlantic and was welcomed in New York by a gun salute from the United States Navy, but all thoughts of a round trip to and from Australia without refuelling were abandoned when coal supplies were discovered in Australia. She worked the Atlantic crossings for many years but is perhaps best known for laying the first telegraph cable across the Atlantic Ocean. Her end was certainly not what Brunel would have expected. She was used as a showboat with a floating circus and funfair at the 1886 Liverpool Industrial and Maritime Exhibition, before being broken up in 1891.

At its height, the Millwall Iron Works employed between 4,000 and 5,000 men. Shipbuilding continued in Millwall until about 1866, by which time competition from the Clyde and Tyne was becoming so strong that the industry came to an end.

There is still much to see. Part of the timber slipway where the great ship was launched has been preserved, as has much of the Millwall Iron Works, now converted to apartments in Burrells Wharf.

Dudgeons were at the Sun Iron Works in Millwall. In 1863, John and William Dudgeon set up in Cubitt Town. They profited from the American Civil War and built fast twin screw blockade runners for the Confederacy. They pitched for a contract to build a warship for the Brazilian government but lost it to Samuda Brothers. Soon after this setback both yards closed, William died, and John never recovered his health.

Joseph D'Aguilar Samuda was born in 1813. In 1830 he joined his brother, Jacob, at an ironworks in Southwark. Samuda's then began building ships at Orchard Place, Bow Creek, before moving to London Yard in Cubitt Town in 1852. Despite setbacks (Jacob was killed in an accident on the *Gypsy Queen*) the firm thrived. They were pioneers of building ships of steel and by 1863 were producing nearly double the output of all other London yards put together. They continued in business until 1885.

In recent years, the Museum of London has excavated the south-east entrance to the West India Docks and uncovered evidence of a seventeenth-century shipyard, Rolt's Yard, and a later yard belonging to Thomas Pitcher.

Yarrows

Alfred Fernandez Yarrow was born in 1842. At the age of 15 he was apprenticed to Messrs Ravenhill, manufacturers of marine engines. A talented youth, he added to his training at Ravenhills by attending scientific lectures, including those given by Michael Faraday. His early life was far from easy; his father went

bankrupt and life for the family was hard. When he completed his apprenticeship, Ravenhills offered him a job at £100 per year with the added comment: 'You had better accept it, for we know exactly the financial position of your father and you cannot do any better.'

But Yarrow wanted to work for himself and turned the offer down. He went into partnership with a Mr Hedley and set up as Yarrow and Hedley at Folly Wall on the Isle of Dogs. Their first order was for a thief-proof door for a safe in a jewellers' shop in Brighton, but eventually they began making steam launches; 350 were built between 1868 and 1875.

The firm soon outgrew Folly Yard and moved to London Yard, a short distance downstream in Cubitt Town. The site was first occupied by the chain cable works of Brown, Lenox & Co. and then the boiler makers and iron works of Westwood, Baillie, Campbell & Co. The yard had a 450ft river frontage and new buildings were built with steel from Sir William Arroll & Co.

Yarrow built launches for torpedo boats. Their first order was from the Argentine and other orders from foreign governments followed. They soon began supplying the Admiralty with a series of high-speed boats – the *Batoon*, the *Hornet* and the *Havcock*. The *Hornet* attained a speed of 27.3 knots. It was powered with water tube boilers, a marked improvement on the previously used locomotive boilers. Then, by using high tensile steel rather than mild steel, the firm was able to reduce the thickness of the ship's hull and so attain still greater speeds. A Yarrow vessel was the first to attain 30 knots.

In 1895, orders for eight destroyers and ten torpedo boats were received from Japan. In their attack on Port Arthur, the Japanese were thus enabled to sink the Russian battleships *Czarevitch* and *Retvisan*. Yarrows therefore played a decisive part in Japan's victory in the Russian-Japanese War of 1904.

In 1907, Yarrows moved to the Clyde, to be replaced in London Yard by C&E Morton, manufacturers of pickles, jam and soup.

Torpedo Boat at Yarrow's. (Courtesy of Tower Hamlets Local History Library)

WHAT IS THERE TO SEE?

MILLWALL IRON WORKS. From Island Gardens DLR, turn right for about 400 yards. John Scott Russell's premises are clearly seen on the left, just past the Ship pub. Next is Burrells Wharf, within which are buildings surviving from the Iron Works.

GREAT EASTERN SLIPWAY. A few yards upstream from Burrells Wharf are the remains of part of the timber slipway from where the Great Eastern was launched.

Blackwall

Blackwall Yard

In the late sixteenth century, Roger Richardson leased from lord of the manor, Lord Wentworth, 'a parcel of ground called Blackwall, extending from Poplar to the landing place there, in estimation 400 yards; also, a parcel of waste ground from the said landing place to a sluice towards the south west in length 614 yards'. The lease later passed to Nicholas Andrews. It was here that Blackwall Yard was built.

Blackwall has a long history of both shipbuilding and repairing and had particular associations with the East India Company. The company unloaded their cargoes here onto smaller vessels which then continued upstream to offload goods in the City at the Legal Quays. In the early seventeenth century, the company's main shipyard was at Deptford, but Blackwall had a greater depth of water and accordingly, William Burrell, the company's shipwright, suggested that a dry dock, for shipbuilding and repair, should be built there. It was known as Blackwall Yard. The yard began shipbuilding in earnest in 1612; their first ship was the *Globe*, launched soon after 1612. Other ships were soon to follow:

Hector, *Thomas*, *New Year's Gift*, *Merchant's Hope* and *Solomon*. Later in the seventeenth century the yard passed to the Johnson family. Henry Johnson was a later member of that family. His grandfather was Peter Pett, who was the navy's architect at the Royal Dockyard.

As well as building ships for the East India Company, Blackwall Yard, in times of national need, built warships for the navy. In 1661, Samuel Pepys, English Admiralty Official, recorded in his diary: 'went to Blackwall to view the dock which is newly made there and a brave new merchantman to be launched shortly called the "Royal Oak"'. The association with the East India Company was never lost, however, and Johnson continued to make ships for them as well as for the navy. The same year that Pepys visited, Johnson commissioned George Sammon of Wapping to 'digg erect new build' a large wet dock of 1½ acres, the first wet dock on the Thames, not, it must be emphasised, for landing cargoes but for the fitting out of vessels. Johnson and his Blackwall Yard thrived; he was knighted in 1679 and later passed the yard to his son, who became MP for Aldeburgh. Pepys made the rather back-handed compliment about him, writing that he was 'an ingenious young gentleman, but above all personal labour, as being too well provided for to work too much'.

The yard later passed to Captain John Kirby and then to the Perry family. Towards the end of the eighteenth century John Perry II enlarged the dock to 8 acres and it became known as the Brunswick Dock, in honour of the royal house of George III. Perry also built the famous Mast House, which allowed a large ship to have its masts lifted in under four hours.

As the years passed there were others who had interests in Blackwall Yard, including John Wells from Deptford, George Green and Robert Wigram. Meanwhile, however, London's system of wet docks for cargo import and export began to be built. The East India Company wanted a dock for themselves, so they purchased Brunswick Dock and between 1803 and 1806, John Rennie and Ralph Walker constructed the East India Dock, two parallel docks for both export and import trade, with the export dock built on the former Brunswick Dock.

View of Blackwall Yard looking towards Greenwich. (J. Boydell, 1750)

Shipbuilding continued at Blackwall and thrived: in 1840 there were 500 men employed, rising to 1,500 by 1866. But by now, ships were being built of iron rather than with wood. Between 1612 and 1866, the Blackwall Yard built 357 wooden ships, 82 of them for the Royal Navy. Their first iron ship was *Superb*.

In 1843, the yard was split into separate firms; Wigrams were based in the western area and Greens in the east. Richard Green also built clippers. The *Challenger* was one of his most famous ships. It was a tea clipper built as a 'challenge' to American clippers which dominated the tea run from China. In 1850, Richard Green exclaimed, 'I am tired of hearing about Yankee clippers and meant to build a ship to beat them.' His wish came true – *Challenger* beat the American *Yankee* by two days.

Wigrams built iron ships and closed in 1876, the site now occupied by the ventilation shaft of the Blackwall Tunnel. Greens continued until 1907, and then three years later amalgamated with Silley Weir to form R&H Green and Silley Weir, ship repairers.

RIGHT: C.J. Mare, Bow Creek.

FAR RIGHT: Thames Iron Works, Bow Creek.

Bow Creek

Thames Ironworks

The River Lea runs into the Thames at Bow Creek. It was to the western edge of the creek, in 1838, that Thomas Ditchburn, a shipwright, and Charles Mare, a naval architect, moved from their yard in Deptford. The site was previously occupied by William and Benjamin Wallis.

The partnership of Ditchburn and Mare was short-lived; the pair argued and Ditchburn went his own way, leaving C.J. Mare in sole control. The other side of Bow Creek was marshy and inhospitable, but Mare saw its potential and expanded his shipbuilding business there, the Essex side of the creek. It was a wise move because soon the North Woolwich Railway arrived, thereby enabling Mare to import raw materials by rail as well as water.

The firm, now known as C.J. Mare & Co., built ships of iron. But it didn't stop making wooden ships. In 1849, it built the wooden paddle steamer *Vladimir* for the Russian government. Ironically, the vessel aided Russia in her war against the British in the Crimea. For P&O, Mare built the *Himalaya*, at 3,438 tons the largest steamer of her day, and *Peru*, described as 'the most perfect steamer ever built on the Thames'. But Mare was getting into financial difficulty and the threat of closure loomed over the yard and the 3,000 men it employed. The day was saved by Peter Rolt, a wealthy timber merchant and a descendent of Phineas Pett, the famous shipwright. The Thames Shipbuilding Company Ltd was duly formed with capital of £100,000 in twenty shares of £5,000 each.

Thames Iron Works. (Courtesy of Newham Local Studies Library)

Building of the HMS *Thunderer*, Thames Iron Works. (Courtesy of Newham Local Studies Library)

Berthed in Portsmouth Historic Dockyard, and still preserved for us to admire and enjoy today is *Warrior*, the first iron-hulled battleship in the world, built at Bow Creek at the Thames Ironworks. The Crimean War exposed the shortcomings of wooden ships, and France was challenging Britain's long-held and jealously guarded naval dominance. Prince Albert, after inspecting French capabilities at Cherbourg, stormed, 'The war preparations of the French are immense, ours are despicable. Our ministers use fine phrases, but they do nothing. My blood boils within me.' It was against this background that *Warrior* was ordered.

The mighty ship, with four vast decks and a crew of 700, was built for speed and firepower. She was steam powered but also had sails for day-to-day use. When under sail her funnels would telescope down to avoid obstructing the sails. She was constructed at Bow Creek, but her engine and boilers came from the firm of Penns in Greenwich. On 29 December 1860, she was launched by First Lord Sir John Pakington and fitted out at nearby Victoria Dock. She was the largest, fastest, and most powerful warship in the world – 380ft long, 58ft beam, 6,000 tons and 1,250 hp – but never fired a shot in anger; no one dared challenge her!

The Thames Ironworks became one of the most important shipbuilding yards in the country, so much so that it was said 'the fleets of Europe were largely launched from the slips at Blackwall'. Vessels were supplied to Germany, Russia, Spain, Turkey, Portugal and Greece. The company also had a civil engineering department that supplied iron for railway bridges and the roofing for the Great Exhibition.

In common with all Thames side shipyards, the company was beset with labour troubles; strikes were common, culminating in a disastrous one in the late 1890s. The firm was later directed by Arnold Hill, who introduced a forty-eight-hour week, a profit sharing scheme and a number of clubs and societies for workers to enjoy. There were science classes, a choral society, art and literature classes, a cycling club, amateur dramatics, a military band, a temperance league and – with lasting effect – a football club, founded and financed by Arnold Hill. In 1900 it became West Ham United Football Club.

The last warship built at the yard was HMS *Thunderer*. With its 13½-inch guns, it was the largest dreadnought afloat. In its later years, the Thames Iron Works supplied iron for Blackfriars and Hammersmith bridges before competition from the shipyards on the Tyne forced its closure.

WHAT IS THERE TO SEE?

The Thames Iron Works was on both sides of Bow Creek. There are derelict premises in Orchard Place.

Rotherhithe

Nelson Dockyard

Nelson Dockyard stood in Rotherhithe, on the south bank of the Thames at Cuckold's Point. The first occupier was John Deane, who built the 34-gun *Mary Galley* in 1687. Well known to William III, Deane returned to Russia with Tsar Peter the Great who visited England in 1698. There, he helped build ships in the Baltic.

Apart from a short period under Marmaduke Stalkartt, the yard was held by the Taylor, Brent and Randall families throughout the eighteenth century. It was John Randall, in 1789, who built *Discovery* for Commander George Vancouver – an exploration vessel that circumnavigated the globe in 1795 and whose captain discovered the Island of Vancouver. Later, the ship was converted to a bomb vessel, equipped with a large mortar to fire explosive shells. The recoil was so great that the hull had to be particularly strong. They were therefore ideal for arctic explorations where ice was an ever-present hazard. Nelson explored the Arctic in 1772 in another converted bomb vessel, the *Carcus*. *Discovery* ended her days off Deptford as a convict hulk!

John Randall's tenure at Cuckold's Point came to an unhappy end in 1802 with his suicide. There was a dispute with the navy board concerning a badly constructed ship, added to which the firm's orders were down, and to compound his problems his workmen went on strike. Matters came to a head when one of his workmen hit him with a block of wood. All this was too much for poor John Randall who went home and flung himself out of a window.

Thomas Bilbe was a later occupier of Nelson Dock. In 1854, he launched the *Orient*, to carry soldiers to fight in the Crimean War. Ships were hauled onto the slipway by a cradle, which originally was steam powered until hydraulic power was installed in 1900. The shipbuilders of Rotherhithe never quite came to terms with the new ships made of iron. In 1866 the last ship was built at Nelson Dock, the *Argonaut*, after which the yard concentrated on repairing ships.

Also in Rotherhithe was John Beatson's Shipbreaking Yard. The most famous ship to have ended her life here was undoubtedly the *Fighting Temeraire*. Immortalised by J.M.W. Turner in the painting that now hangs in the National Gallery, HMS *Temeraire* was a 98-gun ship of the line built at Chatham. She saw service at the Battle of Trafalgar and Turner's romantic, ghostlike depiction of her last voyage, being towed by a steam tug from Sheerness to Rotherhithe, symbolises the transition from the glory of sail to the utilitarian new age of iron and steam.

Brent, in Rotherhithe, built *Rising Star*, influenced in its design by the ubiquitous Richard Trevithick, the first steamship to cross the Atlantic in an east–west direction. Elias Evans was also at Rotherhithe.

WHAT IS THERE TO SEE?

NELSON DOCKYARD. The DoubleTree Hilton Hotel stands at the site. Turn left from Rotherhithe Station, cross the Grand Surrey Canal after 300 yards and turn first left and then right for Rotherhithe Street. Continue for about half a mile to the hotel. Alternatively, catch the C10 bus from Bermondsey Jubilee Line Station.

TUNNELS, RAILWAYS AND CANALS

Tunnels

Brunel's Rotherhithe to Wapping Tunnel

The opening of the docks caused a vast increase in population in East London. There was no river crossing downstream of London Bridge. A lengthy round trip – for instance, as much as 4 miles from Rotherhithe to Wapping – had to be made to get from one side of the river to the other, unless one employed the services of the Thames watermen. Furthermore, the area around the bridge became enormously congested.

In 1798, Ralph Dodd made an ill-fated attempt to build a tunnel between Gravesend and Tilbury. It flooded, and the scheme had to be abandoned. A few years later, the Cornishman Richard Trevithick (famous for inventing the railway locomotive) was offered a considerable sum of money by the Thames Archway Company if he could succeed in building a tunnel under the Thames at Rotherhithe. Despite coming close to success, Trevithick was eventually defeated by a combination of flooding and the soft quicksand beneath the riverbed.

It was left to the French-born engineer, Marc Isambard Brunel, to solve the problem of tunnelling through the soft sand. Brunel was born in 1769. Because of his opposition to the French Revolution he left France for America in 1793. He soon rose to prominence in New York, but then in 1799 came to England to marry, fulfil a Royal Navy contract, and set up as a manufacturer of special boots for the army. Peace with France after the Battle of Waterloo reduced demand for Brunel's boots so much so that the poor man found himself in the King's Bench Prison for debt. Prompted by the Duke of Wellington, the government made £5,000 available to pay off Brunel's debts, which left him free to continue his researches. Brunel now set about solving the difficult problem of tunnelling in soft ground. In 1818, he patented a method for 'Forming Drifts and Tunnels Underground'. His patent proposed a shield, constructed in the form of an iron frame, with a number of individual cells, at the tunnel face. A miner was housed in each cell and at the tunnel face were a series of removable boards. It was the job of the miner to dig out a few inches of earth beyond the board, replace the board and then move to another cell. When all the boards had moved forward the shield would be advanced in the direction of tunnelling and the whole process then repeated. The shield supported the structure of the tunnel until its walls could be secured with brick linings. More details and excellent diagrams are given in Andrew Mathewson and Derek Laval's *Brunel's Tunnel*, and the later book by Kentley, Hulse and Elton which is available from the Brunel Museum.

In 1825, work began to link Rothcrhithe with Wapping on the opposite bank. Brunel had no end of difficulties – he had to contend with floods, strikes, firedamp and men being killed, but he persevered. There were also unwanted visitors. The Thames Tunnel Company encouraged tourists to come at 1*s* a head to provide finance, and even held a banquet, immortalised in a painting by Alan Ramsey. Funding was an ever-present problem, and in 1828 the money ran out and the tunnel was bricked up – causing *The Times* to comment acidly about the 'Great Bore'. But work began again in 1835, and eight years later the tunnel was completed. On 26 July 1843, Queen Victoria, with Prince Albert, arrived on the royal barge to give her seal of approval. In its early days the tunnel was only used by pedestrians, but it was eventually sold to the East London Railway in 1865, who opened it as a railway line from north of the river to New Cross.

The pumps used by Brunel and his resident engineer and son, Isambard Kingdom Brunel, to pump water out of the tunnel during its construction were housed in the Engine House. It was due to be demolished, but was saved by Nicholas Falk and the people of Rotherhithe and is now a museum.

WHAT IS THERE TO SEE?

London Overground trains run through the Rotherhithe to Wapping tunnel; the journey can be experienced first-hand. There is more to see at the **BRUNEL MUSEUM** (see Chapter 18).

Tower Subway

Peter William Barlow's Tower Subway is in grave danger of being lost to history. Barlow (1809–85) was a railway engineer and designer of suspension bridges. It was while he was working on the Lambeth Suspension Bridge (likewise in danger of being forgotten) that he hit on the idea of a tunnel beneath the Thames from the Tower to Bermondsey. He reasoned that the cast-iron cylinders he used to sink vertically into the Thames clay to form the piers of the suspension bridge could just as easily be driven horizontally under the riverbed. As with so many visionary Victorian engineers, seized with a new idea, he dreamt of more ambitious plans and proposed a network of 'omnibus subways' beneath the streets of London, outlining his ideas in a pamphlet published in 1867. Unless the London Underground is counted, his series of subways came to nothing, but the government was nevertheless sympathetic to the idea of a Tower Subway and in 1868 an Act of Parliament was passed for a subway from Tower Hill to the Pickleherring Street and Vine Street junction in Bermondsey.

Understandably, people were sceptical; there were still memories of Brunel's difficulties at Wapping and Rotherhithe, and no real appetite, to use *The Times* newspaper's jibe, for another 'Great Bore'. But the scheme went ahead, and the Tower Subway Company was formed with Peter Barlow as engineer and secretary. He had taken on as a pupil the young James Henry Greathead a few years earlier and worked with him on the Midland Railway. Greathead, of course, went on to great things with the London Underground.

Tunnelling began in 1869 and was completed within the year. The tunnel was 1,340ft long, of which 890ft was below the water at an average distance from the river bed of 30ft. Barlow designed the cutting shield himself and it was made by the Bells Goodman Company at the Walker Engine Works and Foundry in Newcastle upon Tyne. It weighed about 2 tons and was made of wrought and cast iron with a cutting edge of 7ft 2in diameter. Behind the cutting face was a wrought iron faceplate in the centre of which was a doorway (4ft square) which was closed by means of a watertight iron sliding door.

Soil was removed to a length of about 2ft behind the door sufficient for a man to enter and he (and other men) would remove soil from within the shield. Screw jacks then pushed the shield forward and the tunnel was lined with cast iron rings in four segments.

There were vertical shafts at both ends of the tunnel, 10ft in diameter and a 2ft 6in gauge single track railway was installed on which ran a twelve-seater 'omnibus'. It was hauled by a steel cable powered by a stationary steam engine, one on both banks, which also operated the lifts. Passengers paid 2*d* for first class and got priority on the iron cage lifts, while everyone else paid 1*d*. There were no windows in the omnibus and it took 70 seconds to get from one side to the other. Regrettably, it didn't pay and after three months the lifts, track and cable car were removed, spiral staircases installed, and passengers charged ½*d* to walk. Tower Bridge opened in 1894 and within two years the Tower Subway closed.

Nevertheless, interest in tunnels persisted. The first underground railway from Farringdon to Paddington had opened in 1863. It was built using the cut-and-cover method where a trench is cut, the track laid, and the trench covered over again. The difficulty was that property had to be demolished, which was not the case with tunnels. In 1883, plans to build a cable-hauled railway in a tunnel from Stockwell to King William Street in the City were revived with the formation of the Patent Cable Tramway Corporation. They went into liquidation because of persistent failures of the cable haulage. The scheme was rescued when the line was electrified in 1890, and it is now the Northern Line.

As for the Tower Subway, it was used by the London Hydraulic Power Company to carry their pipes, then water mains and now cable TV circuits.

WHAT IS THERE TO SEE?

The tunnel entrance building still stands just below the ticket office at the Tower of London.

The Blackwall Tunnel

Originally, the Metropolitan Board of Works commissioned Sir Joseph Bazalgette to build three tunnels, one each way and the third for pedestrians. Responsibility then passed to the London County Council; Bazalgette's scheme was dropped and the job given to Sir Alexander Binnie.

There are now two carriageways under the river between Blackwall and North Greenwich, but originally there was only one. What is now the northbound tunnel, engineered by Sir Alexander Binnie, opened first in 1897. It was opened by the Prince of Wales and at the time was the largest underwater tunnel in the world, an engineering feat as great as Tower Bridge. But unlike the famous bridge it was unseen, and so has never gained the same degree of acclaim. It was not without human cost – 1,200 people had their homes destroyed to make way for the approach roads. The tunnel had to be cut through water-bearing strata and so a mechanism for holding the water back had to be found. As with Brunel's tunnel between Rotherhithe and Wapping, a shield was employed.

Advances had been made in tunnel construction since Brunel's time. In 1864, Peter Barlow patented a cylindrical shield, which he used for his pedestrian tunnel beneath the Thames at Tower Hill, as described above. J.H. Greathead had been Barlow's assistant at Tower Hill and was resident engineer at Blackwall. He developed an improved version of Barlow's shield. Using this improved shield, the Blackwall project took a mere six months to complete, compared with the eighteen years taken by the Brunels at Wapping. The improved shield came to be known as the 'Greathead Shield' and was also used to dig London's first deep underground railway line, now the Northern Line between Stockwell and Bank.

At Blackwall, as earth was cut away, the shield was pushed forward into the earth by twenty-eight hydraulic rams and – innovatively – compressed air was used in combination with the shield to keep the river water ingress to a minimum. The tunnel was built perilously close to the riverbed, within 5ft at times. This was to keep gradients to an absolute minimum and so reduce the lengths of the approach roads. Tunnelling with compressed air had been pioneered as far back as 1830 and was used at Blackwall to provide a pressure within the tunnel greater than the pressure of water above. The danger was that 'blow outs' could occur if the depth of soil beneath the river was too shallow. To counteract this, a layer of clay was dumped on the riverbed. The unfortunate workmen who had to dig at these high pressures often went down with the dreaded 'bends' – but apparently they got compensation. The southbound tunnel was opened in 1967, dug with a Greathead Shield previously used at the Dartford Tunnel.

Rotherhithe Road Tunnel

Opened in 1908 by the Prince of Wales (the future King George V), the tunnel provides a road link between Rotherhithe and Limehouse. It was built for the LCC by Maurice Fitzmaurice, using the Greathead Shield method in a similar way to the Blackwall Tunnel. A section of the shield can be seen at the tunnel's entrance at both Rotherhithe and Limehouse. The approaches were made by the 'cut-and-cover' method. About 3,000 Rotherhithe residents had to be rehoused, and a significant proportion of the £2 million cost of the project was for this purpose. There is a footpath for pedestrians to walk through, but I would strongly advise against. Despite the fume extraction fans, the noise and pollution are extremely disagreeable. There are also tunnel by-laws, for instance, you can only take your dog through if you are in a car.

Greenwich Foot Tunnel

According to Sir Christopher Wren, 'the best view of Greenwich' is from Island Gardens, the southern tip of the Isle of Dogs; indeed, many would say the best view in London. To begin with, the view was meant not for the people who lived on the Isle of Dogs but for those in the Royal Naval College on the opposite bank. The area was kept free from industrial development so as not to spoil the outlook for the naval officers. The park was created in 1895 as a 'little paradise for local people'. It was opened by Will Crooks, who later became Mayor of Poplar, the first Labour mayor in London.

On the right as one enters the park is the entrance to the Greenwich Foot Tunnel, which replaced the ferry. Will Crooks, best known for his open-air meetings outside East India Dock (later known as 'Crooks' College'), was a fervent campaigner for a free foot tunnel beneath the Thames. Many workmen from Greenwich had to make the daily trip by ferry to work in the docks and the 1d fare was a considerable sum to pay. Apart from the cost savings, a tunnel would allow those living on the island easy access to the fresh air of Greenwich Park and Blackheath. Crooks was successful, and the tunnel was built in 1902 by the

Greenwich Tunnel, Island Gardens.

LCC Engineer, Sir Alexander Binnie. Because of the experience gained at the Blackwall Tunnel, only thirty-six weeks were needed for its construction. It is about 60ft deep and there are lifts at each end. By 1905, 9,000 people were using the tunnel each week.

Woolwich Pedestrian Tunnel has a nice copper dome with lantern and was completed for the LCC by Sir Maurice Fitzmaurice in 1912. Further on is the entrance to the Woolwich Free Ferry.

WHAT IS THERE TO SEE?

THE BLACKWALL TUNNEL, ROTHERHITHE TUNNEL, GREENWICH FOOT TUNNEL and the **WOOLWICH PEDESTRIAN TUNNEL** can all be appreciated *in situ*.

London to Blackwall Railway at Forrests Yard. (Courtesy of Tower Hamlets Local History Library)

Railways

The London and Blackwall Railway – the Fourpenny Rope

In 1836, after the promptings of Sir John Rennie, an Act of Parliament was passed authorising the construction of a railway, 3½ miles in length, from the Minories, north of the Tower of London, to Brunswick Wharf in Blackwall. The promoters wished to exploit the market for the many passengers who travelled by the new steamers to Gravesend, Margate and Ramsgate and all points of the globe from Brunswick Wharf. The railway would also connect the City with the West India and East India Docks. The promoters confidently predicted that 'it will be apparent, even to the most sceptical, that few undertakings embrace more important advantages than the present'. They called their 'great undertaking' the Commercial Railway. It was originally intended that it should start in the City but there were complaints from the City Corporation. By 1839, however, a further Act authorised an extension to Fenchurch Street. By this time the railway was known as the London and Blackwall Railway. It was the first railway requiring houses to be demolished in its path, but it seems those affected were generously compensated – 'compared with which, the exactions of the country gentry were liberal arrangements'.

George and Robert Stephenson were appointed engineers. They built the handsome brick three-arched viaduct (which now carries the DLR) through Limehouse. It can be clearly seen from Limehouse Basin. The early railway engines were not of the conventional variety. Instead, stationary steam engines, at each end of the line, operated ropes that were 7 miles long and wound round drums, which pulled the passenger carriages along. At first the rope was made of hemp and it was not uncommon for it to snap, the recoil causing considerable damage. As if that wasn't enough, the hapless passengers were then required to assist the guard by pushing the coaches to the next station! There were a series of stations en route – Leman Street, Cannon Street Road,

Shadwell, Stepney East, Limehouse, West India Dock, Millwall Junction, Poplar and Blackwall. Fares were *6d* for first class and *4d* for second, giving rise to the popular term for the railway as 'the fourpenny rope'. The journey time from the City to Blackwall was a mere twelve minutes.

The line opened with the usual ceremony on 4 July 1840. The first train set off from the Minories in the City to deliver dignitaries to a grand banquet at the East India Company's warehouse at Brunswick Wharf, where they were served turtle with iced punch, whitebait with champagne, and grouse with claret. The occasion was such a sight to see that the inhabitants of two tenement houses by the line were prompted to remove their roof tiles and poke their heads through to get a better view. When conventional steam trains were introduced, a roof was erected over the Limehouse viaduct to prevent sparks from the engine igniting the wooden ships below. Trains ran at first on a 5ft gauge and changed to standard gauge in 1849. At the same time, the London and Blackwall Railway was extended to connect with the East Counties Railway at Bow. This enabled the railway, built to serve the new Poplar Dock, to link, via the London and Blackwall, with Birmingham and the Midlands from a junction at Chalk Farm. Passenger traffic to Brunswick Wharf was withdrawn by the London and Blackwall Railway in 1926 and the handsome terminus was demolished in 1947 to make way for the building of Brunswick Wharf Power Station.

WHAT IS THERE TO SEE?

The viaduct that carried the London to Blackwall Railway can be clearly seen from Limehouse Basin. It now carries the DLR. From Limehouse DLR walk down Branch Road (to the left of the entrance to the Rotherhithe Tunnel), at the T-junction turn left, then right to arrive at Narrow Street, where you turn left. After a few yards, turn left into Limehouse Basin. The viaduct is ahead.

The Millwall Extension Railway

The Millwall Dock opened in 1868 and it was connected with the railway network from the beginning. An Act of Parliament of the same year authorised a spur from Millwall Junction (on the London and Blackwall Railway) south through the Isle of Dogs and Millwall Dock to 'North Greenwich'. This North Greenwich should not be confused with the present North Greenwich. The North Greenwich terminus of the Millwall Extension Railway was near the present Island Gardens DLR station. Anxiety about the possibility of sparks from locomotives setting fire to grain, timber, ships or buildings in the docks induced the dock company to insist on a horse-drawn railway at first. In time, locomotives were put into service from the southern terminus and then over a 682-yard viaduct to Millwall Dock. The first was *Ariel's Girdle*, which also carried vast numbers of football fans to watch Millwall Rovers. Many came from Greenwich on the ferry. It also carried workmen at *1d* a trip until the LCC built the Greenwich foot tunnel. There was a 15-minute service at the beginning of the twentieth century, but because of competition from buses, the line closed in 1926.

WHAT IS THERE TO SEE?

The brick-built embankment that carried the railway to the south of the Isle of Dogs can be seen at Island Gardens, next to the DLR station.

The North Woolwich Railway

The original intention of the promoters of the North Woolwich line was to connect Woolwich (south of the river) to the railway network. The plan was for a passenger railway to North Woolwich (north of the river) to serve passengers from Woolwich who could take advantage of the ferry to North Woolwich. The scheme gained pace after the East Counties and Thames Junction Railway built a line, 2¾ miles in length, from Stratford to the Thames at Bow Creek. It opened in 1846. One year later, the line to North Woolwich opened, an undertaking by the well-known railway contractors we met at the Royal Docks, Samuel Morton Peto and George Parker Bidder. The extension, from the Bow Creek and Stratford line to North Woolwich, was 2½ miles long and passed to the south of land very soon to be the Victoria Dock. All this activity prompted a local to exclaim: 'how singular to hear the whistle of the locomotive and the clatter of the iron wheels where 12 months since the heron, the plover and the bittern roamed in undisturbed solitude.'

When the Victoria Dock opened in 1855, its western entrance from the Thames (the only entrance at the time) crossed the new railway and in consequence a swing bridge was built to take the railway over it. This arrangement was plainly inconvenient and very soon the line was diverted north of the Victoria Dock, then south at its eastern extremity, to meet up with the old line and thence via Silvertown to North Greenwich. The abandoned old line became known as the Silvertown Tramway. On the new avoiding line, as it was called, there were stations at Victoria Dock Tidal Basin, Victoria Dock, Custom House and Silvertown.

In 1880, the Royal Albert Dock opened with its entrance from the river to the east. It was, however, connected at the west to the adjacent Royal Victoria Dock by a short canal. The North Woolwich line, which would otherwise have blocked the canal's path, had to be taken beneath the canal by a cut-and-cover tunnel. All was well for some fifty years but then the new larger ships passing through the canal began to scrape along the roof of the tunnel, which had to be lowered.

In the 1870s, the Gas Light and Coke Company came to Beckton. To serve this vast undertaking a single line extension was built from Custom House to the works. It was paid for by the gas company with a 1*d* fare each way. Trains ran to synchronise with the shift patterns of the works. Then, the London & St Katharine Dock Company (owners of the Royal Albert Dock) built a line from Connaught Road to Gallions Reach for onward cargo handling from the dock and for passengers travelling on the ocean-going ships berthed at the dock. They also built a hotel, described as 'small, but first class'. Rudyard Kipling knew it and stayed there before embarking for India. It is included in his novel *The Light that Failed*: 'Is it Tilbury and a tender, or Gallions and the docks?'

WHAT IS THERE TO SEE?

THE NORTH WOOLWICH LINE MUSEUM used to stand at the terminus of the North Woolwich line but closed in 2008. The building still stands … but for how long?

The Jubilee Line

Canary Wharf Jubilee Line Station, designed by Sir Norman Foster, is the *raison d'être* for the 16km Jubilee Line extension from central London, which itself prompted further developments in the Docklands. Every time I enter its bowels I feel a bit like Jonah being swallowed by the whale. But this whale's belly is more than a match for its Old Testament counterpart – London Transport boasts that it could accommodate the entire Canary Wharf Tower lying on its side. Its dimensions are vast, and it is really an enormous box sunk into the ground, 280m long and 32m wide. On 29 October 1993, the go-ahead was finally given to London Transport to extend the Jubilee Line (previously known as the

Fleet Line and renamed in 1977 in honour of the Queen's Silver Jubilee) from Green Park to Stratford. It provides a direct link from Docklands to London Bridge and Waterloo mainline railway stations, and improved connections to the Isle of Dogs, Southwark and Bermondsey. Passengers are whisked from platform to street level via three tiers of escalators. The platforms are separated from the track by glass screens, which cut down the noise and draught. Doors in the screens line up to open with those on the train and so improve safety. Fifty-nine six-car trains were specially built for the Jubilee Line, each with a capacity of 1,040 passengers. In 2005, the line was closed for five days to enable the six car trains to be increased to seven and thereby increase capacity. Then, automatic train operation was introduced, so that now thirty trains per hour can run in peak times. Canary Wharf Jubilee Line Station has been voted London's 'most loved' underground station. I agree!

Docklands Light Railway

The Docklands Light Railway was built to connect central London with the new commercial developments at Canary Wharf. It is a franchise, held from 2014 and until 2021 by Keolis Amey, a joint venture between the passenger transport business Keolis and the engineering consultancy, Amey. Keolis are partners in three UK train-operating companies and run the Nottingham Express Transit system. The franchise is awarded by Transport for London and was previously held by Serco.

The Docklands Light Railway (DLR) was built in stages. First were two lines: from Tower Gateway to Island Gardens at the southern tip of the Isle of Dogs and from Stratford to Island Gardens. The trains are fully automated and controlled from a computer centre in Poplar. Where possible they run on disused railway lines such as the viaduct that carried the London to Blackwall Railway, clearly seen from Limehouse Basin. The service began in 1987. Four years later it was extended to Bank Station on the Central Line, the original line to Tower Gateway retained

as an offshoot. In 1997, a line was built from Westferry that ran parallel with the north side of the Royal Docks to Beckton.

At the instigation of Lewisham Council, the line to Island Gardens was extended to Lewisham via intermediate stations, including Greenwich. It opened in 1999. In 2005, a line was built from Canning Town, south of the Royal Docks, to London City Airport. Four years later it was taken beneath the river to Woolwich. Finally, a branch line was built from Canning Town to Stratford. Various proposals for further extensions are under consideration, including a branch to Victoria.

The first line carried about 17 million passengers every year, increasing to 64 million in 2002 and 110 million in 2014.

Crossrail

The Crossrail Act attained royal assent in July 2008 and construction began in May 2009. Crossrail is planned as a 73-mile railway link from Reading in the west, via central London (with a link from Heathrow Airport), to Abbey Wood in Kent and Shenfield in Essex. In December 2018, services to Abbey Wood will begin from Paddington and go via Canary Wharf, Custom House (in Royal Docks), beneath the Thames and thence to Abbey Wood. At the same time, Crossrail is to be renamed 'The Elizabeth Line' in honour of Queen Elizabeth II. One year later the entire line will be open from Reading or Heathrow to Abbey Wood.

Crossrail is owned by Transport for London. In 2014, the contract for its operation was awarded to MTR Corporation for a period of eight years with an option for a further two. When fully operational, new nine-carriage trains will run with frequencies of up to twenty-four trains every hour in both directions.

Crossrail will bring great benefits to Docklands, in particular the developments planned at the Royal Docks, by linking them directly with Woolwich and North Kent. Journey time will be considerably reduced. Paddington to Canary Wharf will be 17 minutes and Heathrow to Canary Wharf 39 minutes.

During excavations of the tunnel in the central section of the line many items of archaeological importance were unearthed, some of which are on display at the London Museum Docklands.

WHAT IS THERE TO SEE?

The new **CROSSRAIL** station at Canary Wharf is east of West India Quay DLR.

Regent's Canal and Limehouse Basin

Also known as the Regent's Canal Dock, Limehouse Basin marks the exit of the Regent's Canal to the Thames. The canal was constructed to link the River Thames at Limehouse with the Grand Union Canal at Paddington, and thus with the countrywide canal system. The canal was the brainchild of Thomas Homer and in 1802 he asked John Rennie to draw up plans. These, however, took a route through central London and proved too costly. Homer was not discouraged and resurrected the idea in

Limehouse Dock and Regent's Canal. (Thomas Shepherd and F.J. Havell, 1827)

1810, this time following a route around the northern limits of London. There were the usual objections and 'an Observer' wrote a pamphlet complaining of 'the permanent interruption to be occasioned by 29 public bridges, rendering useless 72 acres of land, introducing bargemen and others into land otherwise private and the insecurity to the public from persons passing through a line of country for 9 miles at all times of night'. Despite the objections, the project went ahead under the auspices of the Regent's Canal and Dock Company, in collaboration with John Nash and James Morgan.

However, it soon hit problems when superintendent Thomas Homer was found to have embezzled large amounts of the company's money. He fled to Ostend and then to Scotland, but was finally caught, tried, and sentenced to transportation. Nevertheless, a 10-mile stretch of the canal was opened in 1820 with all the usual celebrations. Lord Macclesfield, the president of the company, and his architect, John Nash, who was also the largest shareholder, sailed in much splendour from Maida Vale to Limehouse, before retiring to the City of London for a splendid dinner. But the whole project eventually cost double the original budget and was never a financial success, particularly in view of the soon-to-arrive railway network. The basin was originally intended for barges, but was later increased in size to take ships, including the new iron colliers. Closed in 1969, its owners, the British Waterways Board, converted it to a marina.

Limehouse Cut, completed by Thomas Yeoman in 1770, is almost 2 miles in length and connects the Thames with the Lea Navigation at Bromley by Bow, avoiding the long journey around the Isle of Dogs. It was rerouted to the Limehouse Basin in 1968.

WHAT IS THERE TO SEE?

From Limehouse DLR walk down Branch Road (to the left of the entrance to the Rotherhithe Tunnel), at the T-junction turn left, then right to arrive at Narrow Street, where you turn left. After a few yards, turn left into Limehouse Basin.

FAMOUS VOYAGES

There is a plaque in King Edward VII Memorial Park in Shadwell. It is in memory of Sir Hugh Willoughby, Stephen Borough, William Borough and Sir Martin Frobisher, brave seamen who set sail from near here in the late sixteenth century. It reminds us of the many world-changing voyages from the banks of the Thames.

The Mayflower and the Pilgrim Fathers

The years following the Reformation were turbulent ones in England. Many were persecuted for their faith, both Catholics and Puritans alike. A group of the latter, known to us as the Pilgrim Fathers, had travelled to Holland with the hope of finding religious tolerance there. But their eventual home proved to be far away in the New World of America. They settled first at Leyden in the Netherlands but then sought 'to have the right worship of God according to the simplicity of the Gospel … and to venture across the vast and furious ocean … [that they] might have comfort in the same'. Two ships were commissioned for the heroic voyage, the *Speedwell* and the *Mayflower*.

Christopher Jones was born in Harwich in the late sixteenth century. He was destined to captain the *Mayflower*, the ship that transported the Pilgrim Fathers to a new life and religious

Plaque in memory of sixteenth-century navigators, King Edward VII Park, Shadwell.

Captain Christopher Jones and Pilgrim Fathers Memorial, Rotherhithe.

freedom in America. His father was a mariner and shipwright and Christopher followed in his footsteps. After ten years of marriage his first wife died; he then married a widow, Joan Grey. Jones was a man of some eminence in Harwich and was one of the town's burgesses. By 1611 the family had moved to Rotherhithe, where the parish records of St Mary's Church record the baptisms of four of their children. As well as being her captain, Jones was part-owner of the *Mayflower*. He was an experienced seaman. Before the *Mayflower* embarked on her historic journey, she was engaged in trade within Europe, exporting English cargo, such as wool, and bringing in return commercial cargo to Rotherhithe, in particular cognac and wine from Bordeaux – the scent of wine perhaps explaining why she was later described as 'this sweet ship' by the Pilgrim Fathers. The *Mayflower* was not a new ship and her size and structure is uncertain. The best estimates, based on later calculations, are that her tonnage was probably about 160 tons, 90ft in length, beam of 25ft, 12ft 6in deep, with three masts and square rigged.

The *Speedwell* set sail from Delfshaven in July 1620 and made for Southampton. The departure was described by William Bradford:

So they left that goodly and pleasant city, which had been their resting place near 12 years, but they knew they were pilgrims, and looked not much on those things but lift up their eyes to the heavens, their dearest country and quieted their spirits.

There were some sixteen men, eleven women and nineteen children in the group, originally from North Nottinghamshire, South Yorkshire and Lincolnshire. Their ruling elder was William Brewster, formerly from Scrooby, a village just south of Bawtry, on the road to Retford. Once at Southampton they dropped anchor.

Meanwhile, Christopher Jones and the *Mayflower* set sail from Rotherhithe. Jones was fortunate to have John Clark as first mate. He had twice been to Virginia and had once been captured by the Spanish. Undaunted, he sailed again with Jones.

On 15 August 1620, both ships began their journey. They were not to get far, for the *Speedwell* was not up to the job. She began to leak and so the two ships moored at Dartmouth where repairs were carried out. After eight days the voyage began again. Three hundred miles beyond Land's End, Captain Reynolds, master of the *Speedwell*, reported she was leaking badly and water had to be continually pumped out. There was nothing for it but

to return to England and so the two ships turned tail and sailed back to Plymouth, mooring at the Old Barbican. The *Speedwell* was abandoned at Plymouth, leaving 102 brave souls to crowd onto the *Mayflower*. On 16 September, the *Mayflower* set sail again. It was to be a hazardous voyage. Winter was approaching and halfway across they encountered strong gales. Disaster almost struck when a beam came adrift on the *Mayflower*, but the day was saved by the ship's carpenter who caulked the seams of the beam that the pitching of the ship had opened. Poor John Howland had a lucky escape; he was washed overboard but managed to grab hold of a rope trailing over the bulwark.

Two months were spent at sea, but then on 21 November 1620 land was sighted, and the *Mayflower* dropped anchor in the calm waters of Province Town Harbour. They settled at a place now named Plymouth, reminding them of their last embarkation place in England. But there are also Rotherhithe place names in America – the Jones River, just south of Plymouth, and Clarke's Island in Plymouth Bay, just off the coast of Massachusetts. Jones, of course, did not stay in New England for long and set sail for Rotherhithe in April 1621, where he continued to use the *Mayflower* to transport commercial cargo. He died in 1622 and lies buried in an unmarked grave in St Mary's Rotherhithe's churchyard. In 1965, on the occasion of the present church's 250th anniversary, a plaque was installed in Christopher Jones's memory.

The Northeast Passage and the Muscovy Company

In the early sixteenth century, many in England realised the advantage of exploring new lands as a means of expanding trade, gaining riches and colonising territory. They were particularly influenced by the success of both Spain and Portugal and didn't wish for England to fall behind. One such was Robert Thorne, a British merchant residing in Spain. He tried to persuade Henry VIII that with 'a small number of ships there may be discovered divers new lands and kingdoms which without doubt your grace shall winne perpetual glory and your subjects infinite profite'. Henry did not respond to Thorne's promptings and it was left until the reign of his son, Edward VI, for action to be taken. At that time, the great Italian explorer, Sebastian Cabot, was living in England. He had already ventured to discover the Northwest Passage and now, in his late 70s, Cabot encouraged a search for the Northeast Passage to exploit trade with Asia. Leading men were quickly persuaded for they were concerned about the decline in trade of English woollen cloth; it had almost halved in the three years between 1550 and 1553.

Steps were taken to address these issues by a group of London merchants known as The Company of Merchant Adventurers to New Lands. They later became the Muscovy Company, and wrote: 'The king and his council, finding it inconvenient that the utterances of the comodities of England, especialle clothe, should so much depend on the Lowe Countries and Spaine, and it shall be beneficiall to have a vent some other waies.' As a consequence, three ships were commissioned to search for the Northeast Passage to Cathay. In command of one of these ships was Richard Chancellor, who wrote:

Certaine grave Citizens of London and men of great wisdome and carefull for the good of their Countrey, began to think for themselves, and whereas at the same time one Sebastian Cabota, a man in those dayses very renowned happened to be in London, they began first of all to deale and consult diligently with him … It was at last concluded that three shippes should be prepared and furnished out for the search and discoverie of the Northerne part of the worlde.

Kit Mayers, in his book on the Northeast Passage to Muscovy, describes how Sebastian Cabot, at the ripe old age of 79, was given the job of organising 'the company for the exploration of new lands'. Money was raised from 215 subscribers – including such eminent men as Lord Howard of Effingham and Sir Francis Walsingham – each contributing £25. Three ships were commissioned for the voyage, the *Bona Esperanza*, the *Edward Bonaventura* and the *Bona Confidentia*.

Derbyshire-born Sir Hugh Willoughby was leader of the enterprise. He was captain of the *Bona Esperanza*. The *Edward Bonaventura* was the largest ship in the little fleet at 160 tons. Her pilot major was Richard Chancellor, with Stephen Borough as master. The smallest of the three was the *Bona Confidentia*, at 90 tons.

The little flotilla left Ratcliffe on 10 May 1553 and was cheered as it passed by Greenwich, with a gun salute for good measure. But then progress was pitiably slow. Strong winds hindered them; it took fourteen days to reach the open sea and a further six weeks to leave the coast of East Anglia. Eventually, on 14 July, land on the west coast of Norway was sighted. Willoughby wrote: 'we found little houses, but the people fled away for fear of us.' The fleet then sailed northwards, hugging the coast all the way. All was going fine until they reached the Senja Islands in the far north of Norway. Here they hit bad weather, in Willoughby's words, 'flawes [flows] of winds and terrible whirle winds'. The ships got separated and the two lighter ones were swept away in the ferocious wind, drifting helplessly to an Arctic oblivion. Willoughby and the crews of the *Bona Esperanza* and the *Bona Confidentia* perished in the Arctic cold. They were discovered the following year by Russian fishermen, east of Murmansk in the Kola Peninsula. Willoughby's account of his voyage was found and returned to England.

Richard Chancellor, in the heavier ship, *Edward Bonaventura*, managed to withstand the storm and after it subsided sailed onwards around the northern tip of Norway to reach Vardo, hoping to meet up again with Willoughby. They waited in vain. Here they met a Scottish fisherman who warned against any further adventure. Refusing to be discouraged, Chancellor sailed on and finally reached Dvina Bay in the White Sea. They were fortunate to come across a Russian fishing boat, its men scared to death at the sight of this vast vessel with its 'new-come ghosts'. However, after 'comforting them with signs and gestures' the fishermen offered them supplies. It was now August 1553 and Chancellor, after mooring the *Edward Bonaventura* at the mouth of the Dvina River, set off for Moscow.

Chancellor found the journey 'very long and most troublesome, wherein he had the use of certaine sleds [sleighs], which in this countrey are very common'. It was a journey of 600 miles or more, so he would have been delighted at the end of it when invited to dine with Tsar Nicholas IV the Terrible on a feast of roast swan on solid gold plates. The Tsar was more than willing for trade with England with ships sending wool and receiving furs in return, 'as they may have passage and their merchants shall have free marte with all free liberties through my whole dominions with all kinds of wares to come and go at their pleasure'.

In the summer of 1554, Chancellor returned to England with the Tsar's letter and in the following year the Company of Merchant Adventurers became the Muscovy Company, the first joint stock company benefitting with a monopoly on trade with Russia until 1698.

Captain John Smith and the First English Colony in America

On the bank of the river at Blackwall, just upstream from the basin of the former East India Dock, stands a monument. It was erected in 1928 by the Association for the Preservation of Virginia Antiquities in memory of the founding of the first English colony in America. It was from this spot at Blackwall that three ships set out on a cold December's day with 105 explorers on board, with the intention of founding an English colony in the New World. Among them was an adventurer called John Smith.

John Smith was born in Lincolnshire in 1580. He served in the Low Countries, fighting for the Dutch against the Spanish, travelled in France and the Mediterranean and then joined the Austrians to fight against the Turks. He was awarded a coat of arms showing the heads of three Turks he had killed in battle,

Virginia Settlers' Memorial, Blackwall.

all in the same encounter, but was then taken prisoner and sold into slavery. He managed to escape and returned to England via Muscovy, Poland and Morocco. Back in England in 1604, this soldier of fortune found himself short of money and with nothing to do.

Meanwhile, plans were being formulated to attempt once more to found an English colony in Virginia. Sir Walter Raleigh had tried before but the colony at Roanoke failed with all colonists lost without trace. A charter was sought from King James I by a group of eminent men including former Speaker of the House of Commons and Lord Chief Justice Sir John Popham, the writer and promotor of English colonisation, Richard Hakluyt, Edward Maria Wingfield, Sir George Somers, Sir Fernando Gorges, Sir Thomas Gates and Captain Bartholomew Gosnold.

Prime mover amongst these grandees was Gosnold. He had studied at Cambridge, then the Middle Temple and in 1602 sailed to Cape Cod. He gave Cape Cod its name and he called Martha's Vineyard after his deceased daughter and the wild grapes he found at the island. A charter was duly granted in 1606 to the Virginia Company (sometimes known as the London Company). It was a joint stock company like the Muscovy Company and East India Company. Shares were purchased at a cost of £12 10*s*, giving shareholders the prospect of riches if the venture was successful. The Virginia Company was formed, therefore, both to bring profit to its shareholders and to establish an English colony in the New World. The company was under the direction of its treasurer Sir Thomas Smith with Thomas West, Lord de la Warre, as the largest investor. He later served as governor and gave the state of Delaware its name. The principal aims of the investors were trade, commerce and most important, financial gain. John Smith saw the opportunity as well and invested. The charter specified that a council was to be set up in Virginia which was to be responsible to a Royal Council in London.

The company chartered three vessels – the *Susan Constant*, the *Godspeed* and the *Discovery*. It was the custom, to avoid the long journey around the Isle of Dogs, for ocean-going ships to leave London from Blackwall. And so it was from Blackwall that, in December 1606, 105 brave men set sail for the New World. In overall charge of the sailing was Captain Christopher Newport. He had served under Drake, was an excellent navigator and had been to America before and so was well suited for the role.

Progress was slow at first, due to storms in the English Channel, but by February the convoy was making excellent headway, sailing close to the coasts of France and Spain. A stop was made at the Canary Islands where, for reasons not entirely clear, John Smith was arrested on a charge of mutiny. He was then incarcerated for the rest of the voyage. After taking on provisions and water the fleet set out and by April reached the Caribbean. It was at the small island of Nevis that the company took on more supplies and here gallows were erected for the use of Smith. According to Lauran Paine, 'Captain Smith, for whom they were intended, could not be persuaded to use them.' At last, on 26 April 1607, Chesapeake Bay was reached, and the bold explorers dropped anchor at a place where they found 'clear water, trees and faire meddowes'.

Once they had landed and found a suitable place to settle, a sealed container, which had been in the safe keeping of Captain Newport, was opened. This had been provided at the beginning of the voyage by the Royal Commission in England and within it was listed those who were to serve on the council of the new settlement. The list included Edward Maria Wingfield, John Martin, John Ratcliffe, Bartholomew Gosnold and John Smith. The fact that the commission had specified Smith no doubt helped his rehabilitation. Captain Newport returned to England and brought new settlers in January 1608, and further ones in October. In the early weeks and months many perished but – in large part due to the endeavours of Smith – the settlement survived at Jamestown, the first English colony in America. John Smith published many works about his life in Virginia, including the episode when Pocahontas saved his life. It seems certain that it was Smith's cordial attitude to the Powhatan Native Americans that prevented the Jamestown colony from meeting the same fate as Roanoke.

Martin Frobisher and the Northwest Passage

Martin Frobisher was born in Yorkshire and raised in London. Before his well-known attempts to discover a Northwest Passage to China, he was, to all intents and purposes, a pirate. But a voyage to search for a Northwest Passage became his overriding aim in life. He enlisted the help of Michael Lok, a director of the Muscovy Company, and with Lok's backing, money was raised for the venture. Three ships were commissioned, the *Gabriel*, the *Michael* and a small pinnace. The crew numbered thirty-four in all, with eighteen, including Frobisher, on the *Gabriel* and seventeen on the *Michael*. The skilled seamen and navigators Christopher Hall and Owen Griffyne also sailed. The little party left Limehouse on 7 June 1576 and five days later reached the open sea. After a brief stop at Shetland to repair a leak in the *Michael*, the convoy sailed west. All went well at first, the sea was calm and good progress was made. To supplement their provisions the pinnace was despatched on a mission to catch fish. But then the weather changed, a violent storm erupted and the pinnace and those on board were never seen again. The winds raged for a week before the seas calmed and then after three days the *Gabriel* sighted land. Sailing at a latitude of 61°, they had reached the east coast of Greenland. By then, another furious storm flared up and the *Michael* was separated from the *Gabriel*. Its crew assumed the *Gabriel* was lost and mindful of the fate of the pinnace, discretion proved stronger than valour, and the *Michael* turned around and headed for home, arriving back in London on 1 September.

Meanwhile, the *Gabriel* faced another storm, this time more ferocious than ever. The gale was so strong that the ship was almost submerged, and it was only the skill of Frobisher that prevented disaster. He managed to detach the mizzen mast and the ship was righted. When all was well, the *Gabriel* headed further west to reach Baffin Bay.

The lure of gold was ever on the minds of the voyage's promoters and when the *Gabriel* reached a tiny island in Baffin Bay which they called Little Hall Island, a crew member was sent ashore to hack off a piece of rock. This done, the *Gabriel* continued into a stretch of open water, which Frobisher mistakenly assumed was the north coast of the American continent. It was in fact a bay, between what are now known as Resolution Island to the south and Lok's Land to the north, the present Frobisher Bay. It was here that the native Inuit were encountered. Each was suspicious of the other, even though gifts were exchanged. It was then that five of Frobisher's men set off with a group of Inuit. They failed to return, and Frobisher feared the worst. He managed to capture an Inuit as a kind of bargaining chip to secure their release but all efforts to retrieve the men proved fruitless. There was nothing for it but to return home with the precious rock and captured Inuit on board.

The party reached England on 9 October. The poor Inuit was dead within the year and the piece of rock was given to Lok for further examination. Alchemy was a respectable field of enquiry in Elizabethan days and many were keen on another voyage, this time, rather than a search for Cathay, to bring back more black rock. The Queen herself was seized by the allure of gold, as were many other eminent persons. She put up the vast sum of £1,000 to finance the venture and allowed the mighty 200-ton Royal Navy ship the *Ayde* as flagship. There was plenty of room in its hold for ore! Investors speculated at first that a £20 profit would be achieved per ton of ore retrieved. This rose in the fantasy and excitement to £200 per ton!

The fleet duly left Blackwall on 31 May 1567. Frobisher and the Limehouse-born Edward Hall commanded the *Ayde*. The *Gabriel* and *Michael* were called back into service, with Edward Fenton (later to command the famous *Mary Rose*) captaining the *Gabriel* and Gilbert York, the *Michael*. The crew numbered 120 and included a number of convicts who were meant to remain in the Arctic wilderness and explore; sensibly, they absconded.

First port of call was the Orkney Islands where the natives fled in fright, fearing an invasion. Then, on 4 July, Greenland was reached and Frobisher Bay a little over a week later. Anchor was dropped at Jackman Sound but after a month, no ore was found. They then headed north to the opposite side of Frobisher Bay to the Countess of Warwick Sound and went ashore. Here black rock was found, and miners hacked away to retrieve it.

On 23 August, the party left for England with 200 tons of rock on board and three Inuit for good measure. It was not a happy journey: the weather was appalling, all three ships were damaged and William Smith, the master of the *Gabriel*, lost his life. England was reached on 23 September, the ore was eagerly sent for investigation and a third voyage planned, not this time from London.

The ore was, of course, iron pyrites – 'fool's gold'!

Sir Ernest Shackleton

It was from St Katharine Dock that the famous explorer, Sir Ernest Henry Shackleton, set out for the south Atlantic on 24 September 1921, never to return. Shackleton had ventured to the Antarctic before: he sailed with Robert Falcon Scott in 1901 and made another voyage in 1908, after which he was knighted by King Edward VII. A third expedition was wrecked when its ship, *Endurance*, was destroyed by becoming trapped in pack ice, Shackleton escaping to safety on a lifeboat.

Shackleton's final voyage was on the *Quest*, with many of the crew members who had sailed with him on *Endurance*. Despite suffering a suspected heart attack in Rio de Janeiro, Shackleton insisted on continuing. The *Quest* reached South Georgia on 4 January 1922. The next morning, Sir Ernest Shackleton was dead. He lies buried at Grytviken cemetery, South Georgia.

WHAT IS THERE TO SEE?

There is a **MEMORIAL** to Captain Christopher Jones at St Mary's Church, Rotherhithe. Adjacent is the Mayflower pub. Turn right from Rotherhithe station along Brunel Road. Turn right at Rupack Street and right again at the Ship pub. The church is 100 yards on the left and the pub is adjacent.

In King Edward VII Park in Shadwell, next to the air extractor shaft of the Rotherhithe tunnel there is a **PLAQUE** in memory of Sir Hugh Willoughby, Stephen Borough, William Borough and Sir Martin Frobisher, brave seamen who set sail from near here in the late sixteenth century. Turn right from Wapping Station and right at Wapping Wall for 200 yards. The park is on the right, opposite Shadwell Basin.

There is a **MEMORIAL** to Captain Smith and the Virginia Settlement in Blackwall by Wendy Taylor. From East India DLR, cross Blackwall Way and walk along Newport Avenue ahead. After the road goes left turn right into Jamestown Way. The memorial is on the Thames Path, to the left.

STREET ART, MUSEUMS, FARMS AND DOCKLANDS AT WAR

There is probably nowhere in the country to rival London's Docklands for its street art; wandering around you will find a lot of examples. The following are a few of my favourites.

On the north bank, a few yards downstream from Tower Bridge, is David Wynne's *Girl with a Dolphin*. It dates from 1973 and has a twin, *Boy with a Dolphin* in Cheyne Walk, Chelsea. David Wynne never went to art school and wasn't really accepted by the art establishment. But he was accepted by the royal family, for whom he worked, and also by the Beatles, to whom he introduced the Maharishi Mahesh Yogi. In answer to his critics, Wynne replied, 'nobody yet has erected a statue to a critic and I doubt anyone ever will'.

A few yards further on is Wendy Taylor's *Time Piece*. Trained at St Martin's School of Art, she also did *Rope Circle* in London Dock's Hermitage Basin (see *Chapter Six: London Dock*) and the *Virginia Settlers Memorial* at Blackwall (see *Chapter 17: Famous Voyages*) and *Spirit of Enterprise* at the west end of the South West India Dock.

Adorning the west portal of the Limehouse Link is Yemeni-born Zadok Ben-David's *Restless Dream*. It shows a multitude of figures swirling about in a haphazard and uncoordinated manner. He was at the University of Reading and St Martin's School of Art. He was commissioned for work at the Beijing Olympics.

Standing opposite the Grapes pub in Limehouse is London-born Jane Ackroyd's *Herring Gull* (see *Chapter 20: Docklands Pubs*). Also in Limehouse, a few yards north of Westferry DLR station, is Peter Dunn's and the Art of Change's *Dragon Gate*. It celebrates the fact that Limehouse was once London's China Town. Peter Dunn also did a series of murals in association with those protesting against the changes, post-1980, on the Isle of Dogs. They are now in the Museum of London Docklands.

The famous Sir Richard Westmacott sculptured the statue of *Robert Milligan* on West India Quay (see *Chapter 5: West India Dock*) in front of the Docklands Museum. Probably the best-known sculptor of his day, Westmacott did *Achilles* in Hyde Park and the pediment at the British Museum, the *Rise of Civilisation*.

Glasgow-born Bruce McLean studied (more rebelled) at St Martin's School of Art. His great love of jazz is reflected in the jazzy railings at the entrance to Cabot Square from the floating footbridge over the West India Import Dock (see *Chapter 5: West India Dock*) and in a painting in the Bull's Head Jazz pub in Barnes. A little further on in Cabot Square is Richard Chaix's *Twin Figures* and the fountain in the middle of the square.

On the riverbank, between Limehouse and the Isle of Dogs, is Constance de Jong's *Speaking of the River*, a bench that when sat on

LEFT: *Restless Dream* by Zadock Ben-David, Limehouse Link.

Below (L-R): *Herring Gull* by Jane Ackroyd, Limehouse.
Dragon Gate by Peter Dunn, Limehouse.
Robert Milligan, West India Quay.

relates a commentary of the area. Regrettably it was not working when I was last there.

Everyone's favourite is Pierre Vivant's *Traffic Light Tree*, now moved to Trafalgar Way, the eastern exit road from Canary Wharf. It was described thus by Pierre himself, 'The Sculpture imitates the natural landscape of the adjacent London Plane Trees, while the changing pattern of the lights reveals and reflects the never-ending rhythm of the surrounding domestic, financial and commercial activities.' Nearby, by the north-east corner of Poplar Dock (see *Chapter 5: West India Dock*), is *Figure Head* by Anna Bissett. Also, here are splendid Stothert and Pitt Travelling Cranes.

In Stewart Street, a little south of the Blue Bridge on the east side of Isle of Dogs, is John Outram's Storm Water Pumping Station. Much praised and something of an architectural classic, the function of the building is to receive storm water, drained from the Isle of Dogs, in an underground chamber, and then pump it to a surge tank from where it flows by gravity to the Thames. Hidden inside is a tank, control room and an electric pumping chamber. But it is the outside that attracts. Completed by John Outram in 1988, it is full of colour and jolly good fun, winning a Civic Trust Award in 1989. Outram tells us his design is a 'temple to summer storms'. The design shows a river flowing from a cave (the fan, whose function is to expel any build-up of methane gas). It surges down the walls of blue brick between tree trunks (the large round central columns) on either bank. Built to last 100 years, it is designed to be earthquake, explosion and vandal proof.

Halfway along the north side of Greenland Dock is a bust of James Walker by Michael Rizzello. A nephew of Ralph Walker of West and the East India Dock fame, James Walker was born in Scotland and worked with his uncle before becoming chief engineer of the Commercial Dock Company in 1808. Michael Rizzello was British born of Italian parents. He also did the Stave Hill Map, a map of the docks as they were in 1896, on top of the Stave Hill Mound in Rotherhithe's Ecological Park. It is best to visit after a shower of rain because the map is sculpted to allow the docks to

Traffic Light Tree, by Pierre Vivant.

James Walker by Michael Rizzello, Greenland Dock.

Storm Water Pumping Station by John Outram, Stewart Street, Isle of Dogs.

The Navigators by David Kemp, Hay's Galleria, Bermondsey.

fill with water. Further along Greenland Dock and north of the splendid wrought-iron Swing Footbridge, is the Lakes. Most of the timber for the Surrey Docks was imported from Scandinavia, and the Lakes is an ingenious housing scheme that evokes this part of the world. It is by Shepheard Epstein and Hunter and was built in 1989 over the filled-in Norway Dock.

In Rotherhithe, as well as memorials to Captain Jones and Lee Boo (see *Chapter 19: St Mary's Church, Rotherhithe*) there is a sculpture in a small park by Peter Mclean, *Sunshine Weekly and Pilgrim's Pocket*, showing a Pilgrim Father watching over a small boy reading about the New World in the *Sunshine Weekly* Newspaper.

At the riverbank, just upstream of the Angel Pub, the memory of Dr Alfred Salter is kept alive with a piece of sculpture by Diane Gorvin entitled *Dr Salter's Daydream*. Dr Salter was a Quaker and Bermondsey's first Labour MP. He was born in Greenwich in 1873 and fought all his life to improve the living conditions of local people. In 1928, he was successful in getting the pleasant public housing built by Culpin and Bowen, just to the south of Cherry Garden Pier, to replace 'the death traps and fever dens' prevalent in Bermondsey before. After qualifying at Guy's Hospital, he set up in practice in nearby Jamaica Road, charging a mere *6d* per consultation, much to the annoyance of his medical colleagues. He first served on Bermondsey Borough Council in 1903, as did his wife, Ada Brown. And it was Ada, Mayor of Bermondsey in 1922, who was to announce the election of her husband as Bermondsey's first Labour Member of Parliament in that same year.

Within Hay's Galleria is another great favourite: *Navigators* by David Kemp is a very large bronze and steel kinetic sculpture. David Kemp, a Londoner, went to sea in the Merchant Navy before training at Wimbledon Art School. He now lives in Cornwall. David Kemp tells us he built *Navigators* way back in the yuppie daze of 1986.

In the middle of the undeniably striking and quirky Circle in Elizabeth Street (off Shad Thames) is *Jacob*, the statue of a dray horse by Shirley Place. It was landed here by helicopter.

Jacob commemorates the Courage Brewery dray horses that were stabled nearby. Shirley Place tells us it was her intention 'to portray the dignified tolerance and the power of these horses plus a hint of resignation to man's direction and the vagaries of a cold wet windy winter'. She has certainly captured it perfectly, as you will see should you be here between the months of November and February.

The Museum of London Docklands, West India Quay

The magnificent museum occupies one of the fine, Grade I listed warehouses on West India Quay. It grew out of collections accumulated by the Museum of London and Port of London Authority, the latter provided when the inner docks closed. Support from the LDDC, the Heritage Lottery Fund and others enabled Chris Elmers and Bob Aspinall to make the vision of a Museum of Docklands a reality. Exhibits are arranged broadly in chronological order, beginning at the top of the building and working down. The first gallery explains the work that went on in the many warehouses, transit sheds and wharves that lined the riverside and docks. There are exhibits of handling barrows, scales and other weighing equipment, apparatus to transfer goods from the quayside to the loop-hole doors on the many levels of the warehouse and much more.

A gallery is devoted to explaining the inextricable link between sugar imports from the West Indies to the West India Dock and the slave trade. Well-known men associated with building the docks also had interests in transferring West Africans to the Caribbean to work on plantations owned, in many cases, by the same men. This obnoxious trade was ended in 1807, when enlightened Christians like William Wilberforce persuaded the British government to end the Atlantic slave trade. It ended completely throughout the British Empire in 1833. Significantly, the gallery opened in 2007, 200 years after Wilberforce was successful in getting Parliament to act.

The important part the River Thames has played in London's history is emphasised, as well as the life of communities on its banks. Wapping, Limehouse and Shadwell are highlighted in a gallery called Sailor Town, where all sorts of activities associated with the river trade are described.

Labour problems in the port are explained, in particular the Dock Strike of 1889 when men fought for and got their 'dockers' tanner'. The many vessels that entered the docks are detailed, from sail to steam and from timber to iron.

Docklands at War tells how the docks suffered badly in the Second World War. Night after night they were pounded by the German Luftwaffe. It began on 'Black Saturday', the afternoon of 7 May 1940 and continued for thirteen weeks. But London's Docks never closed. Much of the war effort came from docklands: the sugar manufacturer, Tate & Lyle, made parts for aircraft; the cable companies supplied pipe lines under the ocean (PLUTO) to carry fuel for the Normandy Landings and the Allied advance through France. Mulberry Harbours were constructed in the East India Dock for floating harbours at Normandy, and boats from the Thames sailed out to Dunkirk to play their part in the evacuation of Allied soldiers.

The epic changes, many not welcome, in the Isle of Dogs and elsewhere are outlined with the coming of Canary Wharf and all that followed. The museum ends at the Sainsbury Centre, a study area and archive.

The Brunel Museum, Rotherhithe

The museum (turn right from Rotherhithe station along Brunel Road; turn right at Rupack Street and right again at the Ship pub; turn left at the church and then right for the museum) is housed in Isambard Kingdom Brunel's engine house, where once were kept the pumps used to pump Thames water out of his and his father's famous tunnel. The museum tells the story of the tunnel and of other works of the famous father and son team. Inside is a John Rennie steam engine, a video story of the tunnel and other helpful displays. Outside is a pump used at Lavender Dock before it closed. The tunnel is described in the section on tunnels (see *Chapter 16*).

Docklands Countryside and Farms

In the heart of Cubitt Town is Mudchute Park and Farm (turn left from Island Gardens DLR along Manchester Road for about 500 yards, then left along Pier Street to the farm). An oasis of countryside in the heart of Docklands, Mudchute was named by islanders after the mud and silt that was dumped here when the Millwall Dock was constructed. It became a haven for wildlife.

However, in the 1970s, its existence was threatened by the prospect of a high-rise housing development. The locals objected and formed the Mudchute Association to keep the developers away. Soon farm animals were introduced and it wasn't long before Mudchute became the largest urban farm in London. There is a wide variety of farm animals here, including llamas and alpacas. As well as the animals, there is an education centre, a riding school, nature trail, shop and café. Mudchute was, at one time, the home of Millwall Football Club during their early days on the island. In 1890, they opened a stand with a capacity for 600 fans, and a second one followed seven years later.

Surrey Docks Farm was started about thirty-five years ago by two dedicated gardeners, Hilary Peters and Ken Bushell, who wished to bring nature back to London. Originally next to

Mudchute City Farm.

Greenland Dock, the farm moved to its present site in 1986. Now more than 2 acres in extent, it is a pleasant haven where visitors, and local children, can learn about food production and farming. There are cows, donkeys, sheep, pigs, hens and goats, all farmed organically. As well as animals, it has a vegetable and herb garden. (Take the 81 bus – Waterloo to Peckham, alight at Downtown Road; or C10 – Victoria to Canada Water. Alight at Bryan Road/ Surrey Docks Farm.)

Two World Wars

The First World War delayed the PLA's ambitious plans for modernisation. All river dredging was halted, and the construction of the great King George V Dock was put on hold. German bombs fell on the docks from May 1915 onwards, but damage was limited. In fact, far greater damage was inflicted in Silvertown and the adjacent Royal Victoria Dock when the factory of Brunner Mond exploded in 1917.

The Second World War was altogether different – damage estimated at £13.5 million was incurred by the PLA. At the beginning of the war, magnetic mines were dropped in the Thames estuary. They were to prove treacherous to shipping until the Royal Navy eventually developed techniques to deal with them. The docks were a prime target for German bombers. In September 1940, the Blitz began. For fifty-seven consecutive nights, London and the port were bombarded by wave after wave of German aircraft. The worst day was Saturday 7 September, when bombing caused the fiercest fire in London since the Great Fire in 1666. The Surrey Docks suffered particularly badly.

On one dreadful night, 350,000 tons of timber were destroyed in the largest fire ever to occur in Britain. 'Send all the bloody pumps you've got; the whole bloody world is on fire' was the desperate call from the fire officer in charge. The fire broke out in Quebec Yard. It is described vividly in Stuart Rankin's *History of the Surrey Commercial Docks*. He quotes the account of PLA official T.L. Mackie:

> The day light exposed a terrible scene; the greater part of the timber docks, like a barren smouldering wilderness and huge warehouses completely gutted. Ships which only a few hours ago had been discharging cargoes were torn by the blast and defaced by fire … Steel girders were twisted to indescribable shapes. Alas, this shambles proved to be more than unsightly wreckage, for the bombs and fire had claimed toll of human life, and the bodies still lay among the charred debris.

As many as 400 people lost their lives in one night alone. Another night saw the destruction of seven of the Gwilts' magnificent warehouses, which lined the West India Import Dock.

As well as being on the receiving end of bombing raids, the port also played its part in the war effort. Ships from the port were involved in the Dunkirk evacuation and the docks themselves were used for the repair and fitting-out of warships. The giant Maunsell Bombardment Towers were built at the Surreys before being towed downstream to stand guard at the Nore against enemy attack from the estuary. Both the East India Import Dock and the South Dock of the Surrey complex were emptied and used for the construction of Mulberry Harbours, ready for the D-Day landings.

DOCKLANDS CHURCHES 19

St George in the East, Wapping

St George in the East, the Highway.

St George in the East, the Highway, interior.

churches to be built in and around London to serve the increasing population and to discourage the spread of dissenting churches. In the event, only twelve were built, one of which is Nicholas Hawksmoor's St George in the East. The architectural historian, Nikolaus Pevsner, calls it 'the most original of Hawksmoor's East End churches'. The master mason was Edward Strong Jr. Its noble 160ft tower, with an octagonal lantern on top, is a distinctive local landmark. In the mid-nineteenth century, the church found itself at the centre of anti-Catholic demonstrations caused by the perception that the rector, Bryan King, was introducing too much ritual into services. There were fistfights, the police were often called, and it even led to the church being closed for two Sundays. Poor Bryan King was accused of 'Popish innovations', but, from a letter a 'layman' penned to the Bishop of London, he seemed a distinct improvement on his predecessor:

The surprise here is that this is a church within a church. It was badly bombed in the war, and the interior was reconstructed in 1964 and a smaller church inserted within. The church, as seen by passing traffic thundering along the Highway, was built following the New Churches Act of 1711. This Act planned for fifty new

During the last seven years of the late rector's incumbency, he only appeared once in his parish church … the present rector (Bryan King) has been ever constant in his attendance to his duties, save only for those few months, when through broken health, caused by the persecutions, to which he has been subjected, he was compelled to seek a brief period of repose … the late Rector altogether neglected the duty of parochial visitations and superintendence. Mr King has established two mission chapels, five or six schools, affording religious instruction to upwards of 600 children, and a penitentiary for reclaiming fallen women.

King's health finally broke down, causing him to leave the parish for calmer waters at Avebury.

Henry Raine, founder of Raine's Foundation School, lies buried in the churchyard and he and his family are commemorated with a pyramidal monument to the east of the church. Henry Raine's school stood in Raine Street, a little to the south. It can be identified by nice figures of a boy and girl to the front. The school educated fifty boys and girls and provided them with clothing. But Henry Raine went further and set up a charity whereby, twice a year, a £100 marriage portion was given to any girl in service who was formerly a pupil at the school and who intended to marry 'an honest and industrious person' resident in the parish of St George in the East, or in the neighbouring parishes of Wapping or Shadwell. The girls had to be at least 22 years of age and able to provide a certificate of 'good behaviour and industry during six years servitude' from their master and mistress. Many girls applied. The lucky winner was chosen by lottery, and was presented with a bag of 100 sovereigns amidst great celebration. Raine House became the offices of the Academy of St Martin in the Fields, the orchestra founded by Sir Thomas Mariner in 1959, and is now a community centre.

To the rear and east of the church, at the far end of the churchyard, is the former mortuary, which, as the inscription shows, in 1904 became the Metropolitan Borough of Stepney Nature Study Museum. It once housed fifty tanks of fish, a butterfly collection, a beehive and the body of an Indian bee-eating bird found in a consignment of tea bound for St Katharine Dock. The museum was opened by the rector of St George in the East for the benefit of local children. It closed in 1939.

WHAT IS THERE TO SEE?

ST GEORGE IN THE EAST is on the Highway, on the corner with Cannon Street Road. Turn left and immediate right from Wapping Station and walk along Wapping Lane to reach the Highway. The church is on the opposite side of the road.

St Mary Graces, Wapping

St Mary Graces was founded in 1349 by Edward III as a competitor to Westminster Abbey, allegedly in thanksgiving for being saved from drowning at sea. It was built on land that the Romans had used for quarrying gravel and excavated when the Royal Mint was converted to offices. The remains survive of St Mary Graces Church, the chapter house, infirmary, cloisters and many other buildings. Sometimes known as East Minster, it was the last Cistercian abbey to be founded before the Dissolution and was modelled on Fountains Abbey in Yorkshire. Dissolved by Henry VIII in the 1530s, it was used from 1560 onwards as a victualling yard for the Royal Navy. When the Navy moved to Deptford in the mid-eighteenth century, it was used successively as a bakehouse, cooper's workshop and government warehouse, before it was demolished to make way for the Royal Mint.

WHAT IS THERE TO SEE?

ST MARY GRACES. Leave Tower Hill underground station and turn sharp left. Pass to the left of the remains of the medieval city wall. Cross the road (The Minories), turn right and right again, pass in front of Sceptre Court. Cross the road ahead and turn left along East Smithfield past the high brick wall. To your left, and below ground level, are the remains of St Mary Graces.

St Peter's, London Docks

St Peter's is a must for all admirers of the Anglo-Catholic persuasion. Despite the riots at St George in the East, prompted by the introduction of ritualistic Catholic practices, Charles Lowder was not deterred and founded a mission church from St George in the East in Wapping Lane. Lowder was quick to realise that the wealth and prosperity dockers brought to the nation did not extend to their homes in Wapping, where poverty and crime were rife. In 1856, Lowder founded the Society of the Holy Cross, bringing missionary priests to the area to work amongst the poor. Their life was austere and their days long, often 6.15 a.m. to 10.15 p.m. Lowder faced much criticism, particularly for his Anglo-Catholic approach, but during a particularly intense cholera epidemic he finally won over the local people when, without fear for their own safety, his priests tended the sick and saw to their needs. It was at this time that he became known as 'Father' by the people of Wapping – the first Anglican priest to be so-styled. Lowder died in 1880, but trouble persisted. In 1883, a petition was signed by 1,700 evangelical clergymen to the Lord Bishop of London against the institution of his assistant, A.H. Mackonochie, to the benefice of St Peter's, because of his ritualistic practices at St Alban's Holborn.

Lowder's church was built in 1865 but suffered much damage in the war. There is a large wheel window, high up at the east end, placed there to make it visible above the high dock walls and so gain the attention of the dockworkers within. The interior is of red and black brick and typically Anglo-Catholic in style.

WHAT IS THERE TO SEE?

ST PETER'S London Docks is in Wapping Lane. Turn left and immediate right from Wapping Station and walk along Wapping Lane to reach the church after about 200 yards, on the right.

St Paul's, Shadwell

The present St Paul's Church is the third to be built on the site. It has a fine stone steeple and is a Waterloo church built by John Walters with part of the £1 million granted by Parliament as an offering of thanks for the delivery of the country from the threat of Napoleon. Classical in style, it has a tower and a fine steeple.

Captain James Cook was a parishioner at St Paul's and lived in Shadwell with his wife Elizabeth Batts. Cook founded a group of almshouses, which used to be south of the church, and his son James was baptised at St Paul's. There are American connections at St Paul's. It was here in 1720 that Jane Randolph, daughter of Jane Rogers of Shadwell and Isham Randolph, a merchant sailor from Virginia, was baptised. The family moved to America, and in 1739 Jane married Peter Jefferson. In 1743, their son Thomas Jefferson was born, later to become the third President of the United States. His early home was the Virginian plantation of Shadwell!

The scientist William Perkin was baptised at St Paul's and was an active parishioner. In common with so many scientists, William Perkin was inspired by lectures given by the great Michael Faraday. He recorded in 1852, as a young boy of 14, that he 'sat up in that gallery an eager listener to lectures by that great man [and] I little thought then that in four years' time I should be the fortunate discoverer of the mauve dye.' He fell under the spell of chemistry, writing: 'a young friend was good enough to show me some chemical experiments; amongst these were some on crystallisation, which seemed to me a most marvellous phenomenon: as a result, my choice was fixed and it became my desire to be a chemist.' In the evenings and in any spare time he could find he worked away in a crude laboratory he had set up in a back room of his home in Cable Street. There he oxidised aniline (containing toluidine impurities) with potassium dichromate and got a messy black solid, which to his surprise, when dissolved in alcohol gave a purple solution capable of dyeing fabric and remaining colour fast even when exposed to bright light.

Perkin's raw material was coal tar, available in abundance as a by-product from London's gasworks. His discovery heralded a new industry. Mr Punch explains:

There's hardly a thing man can name
Of beauty or use in life's small game
But you can extract in alembro or jar,
From the physical basis of black coal tar:
Oil and ointment, wax and wine,
And the lovely colour called aniline:
You can make anything from salve to a star
(If only you know how) from black coal tar.

There is a laboratory dedicated to Perkin's memory at the Royal College of Science (now Imperial College). William Henry Perkin – the founder of the coal tar industry – was knighted in 1906.

John Wesley preached one of his last sermons at St Paul's. His journal tells us: 'St Paul's, Shadwell was still more crowded in the afternoon, while I enforced an important truth "One thing is needful" and I hope may even resolve to choose the better part.'

WHAT IS THERE TO SEE?

ST PAUL'S CHURCH is on the Highway. Turn left and immediate right from Wapping Station and walk along Wapping Lane to reach the Highway. Turn right and the church is 250 yards on the right.

St Anne's, Limehouse

St Anne's Church, Limehouse.

In common with St George in the East, St Anne's, Limehouse, is another of the fifty new churches provided for by the New Churches Act of 1711. Once again it is by the 'Master of the Baroque', Nicholas Hawksmoor, and some say it is his finest church. The Grade I listed building has a striking west tower, with vestibules, pediments and rusticated quoins. It has an apse to the entrance front and an octagonal top with a clock, said to be the highest in London. Edward Strong, who also worked with Wren at St Paul's Cathedral, served as master mason. It was consecrated in 1730 when, as we are told, 'the bishop drank a little hot wine and took sweetmeats after which the clergy and laity scrambled for the rest and left not a bit'. The church fell victim to a disastrous fire in 1850. It was successively restored by Philip Hardwick (of Euston Station and St Katharine Dock fame), Hardwick's pupil, Arthur Blomfield, and finally in our own day by Julian Harrap. The main body of the church has arched windows above and square ones below. Inside is a prize-winning organ, which was displayed at the Great Exhibition of 1851, and brilliantly coloured glass in the east window. Outside, in the churchyard, is a pyramidal structure with the Wisdom of Solomon inscribed in English and Hebrew. The War Memorial by Arthur Walker (who also did the Florence Nightingale memorial in Waterloo Place) has a vivid relief of scenes from the trenches of the First World War.

ST ANNE'S Limehouse is on the Commercial Road. Turn north from Westferry DLR along Salter Road, bear left along the main road that soon becomes Commercial Road. The church is on the left before the bridge carrying the Limehouse Cut.

Christ Church and St John, Isle of Dogs

Paid for by William Cubitt, it was designed by Frederick Johnstone and was partly built, it is said, with stones from London Bridge. If it is open, the inside is well worth a look. There are many High Church features taken from the demolished church of St John, which used to stand about half a mile to the north. Above the chancel arch is a mural depicting The Company of Heaven. There is a fine pulpit, with its panels decorated with a painting in the Pre-Raphaelite style – *The Annunciation* – and around the walls are the Stations of the Cross.

CHRIST CHURCH AND ST JOHN is on Manchester Road. Turn left from Island Gardens DLR for 200 yards. The church is on the corner with Glenaffric Avenue.

St Mary, Rotherhithe

There used to be a medieval church here, but by the early eighteenth century it had fallen into disrepair and was prone to flooding from the nearby River Thames. Money was raised for a new church, which was begun by John James in 1714. The distinctive west tower was added in 1747 by Lancelot Dowbiggin and is surmounted by a balustrade, above which are slender Corinthian columns and an obelisk spire. William Butterfield carried out an extensive restoration in the nineteenth century.

St Mary's Church, Rotherhithe.

The church is usually open, but for reasons of security can only be viewed through glass panels to the rear of the nave. The roof of the nave is supported by Ionic columns of wood encased in plaster, and there is a fine eighteenth-century reredos at the east end by Joseph Wade, King's Carver at the naval dockyard at Deptford. The communion table and two chairs are from HMS *Temeraire*, broken up at nearby Batson's Yard and immortalised by J.M.W. Turner. The church has many memorials to Rotherhithe seamen, including Christopher Jones, master of the *Mayflower*, who sailed to America in 1620 with the Pilgrim Fathers. There is also a memorial tablet to Peter Hills, who founded the school on the other side of the road.

In the churchyard to the west of the tower are two important memorials, to Captain Christopher Jones, and to Lee Boo, a Polynesian prince. The epitaph on his tomb, written by Brook Watson, Member of Parliament and latterly Lord Mayor of London, reads:

Stop, Reader, stop! Let Nature Claim a Tear,
A Prince of Mine, Lee Boo, Lies Buried Here.

Lee Boo's story begins with Captain Henry Wilson, a Rotherhithe man, and master of the East India Company's ship *Antelope*, who set sail from Falmouth in 1782. Disaster struck on 9 August 1783 when the *Antelope* ran aground and was wrecked off the Pelew Islands, north-east of Indonesia. Wilson expected trouble from the natives and even feared cannibalism, but his fears were groundless. Not only were the Pelew Islanders friendly, but they also took most kindly to the ship's dog, Sailor, having never seen a furry four-legged creature before. In time, Wilson repaired his ship and was ready to return to England. He was implored by Abba Thule, the local king or Rupack, to take with him his eldest son, Prince Lee Boo, for an English education. Lee Boo duly returned and lived with Wilson and his family in Rotherhithe. But his time here was short – he arrived in England in July 1784, but by December he was dead from smallpox, aged only 20. Nearby Rupack Street is named in his memory. Samuel Taylor Coleridge was to write ten years later:

My soul amid the pensive twilight gloom
Mourn'd with the breeze, O Lee Boo! O'er thy tomb

Nearby is a memorial to Christopher Jones, in the shape of a figurehead, by Jamie Sergeant. It was placed here to commemorate the 375th anniversary of Jones's famous voyage to the New World in 1620 as captain of the *Mayflower*. Preparations are already underway in Rotherhithe for the 400th anniversary in 2020.

WHAT IS THERE TO SEE?

ST MARY'S CHURCH, Rotherhithe. Turn right from Rotherhithe station along Brunel Road. Turn right at Rupack Street and right again at Ship pub. The church is 100 yards on the left.

St Olav's Church, Rotherhithe

St Olav is the patron saint of Norway, and the church was built in 1927 to serve the large numbers of Norwegian seamen who came to the Surrey Docks with their shiploads of timber. It is now a second home to Norwegians living, studying or working in London. It also commemorates the many Norwegian seamen who lost their lives in the First World War.

From 1692, when the first Norwegian congregation was founded, until the early nineteenth century, Norwegians worshipped at the Templum Dano–Norvegicum in Wapping. Then in 1871, the foundation stone of the Ebenezer Church for Norwegian seamen was laid by Crown Prince Oscar of Sweden.

John Seaton Dahl was the architect of the present church and the foundation stone was laid by Crown Prince Olav (King Olav V to be). It is entered through the beautiful St Olav's Square, laid out as a garden. The church is built in the English Renaissance style and the copper spire, modelled on the spire at Oslo Cathedral, is crowned with a Scandinavian ship's weather vane. But such was the ferocity of the storms in 1987 that it blew down. The then-rector came to the rescue, however, by raising funds for its restoration by taking part in the London Marathon. As well as a spiritual centre for London's Norwegian community, St Olav's is very much a social centre. One enters the reading room, where food and drink is on hand from a kiosk selling all sorts of Norwegian products, plus Norwegian newspapers and even a television with Norwegian TV channels. Beyond is the nave, with a model of a sailing ship suspended from the roof in true Norwegian tradition.

WHAT IS THERE TO SEE?

ST OLAV'S NORWEGIAN CHURCH. Turn right from Rotherhithe station along Brunel Road. Just past Rupack Street, cross with great care the main road from the Rotherhithe Tunnel. The church is ahead.

DOCKLANDS PUBS

Dickens Inn, St Katharine Dock

The Dickens Inn stands within St Katharine Dock. Built in 1799, it predates the dock and was originally built as a spice store. It was moved on rollers, some 50 yards to its present position, and opened by Charles Dickens's great-grandson in 1976, who commented 'my great grandfather would have loved this inn'. It has been restored in the style of a three-storey balconied inn of the eighteenth century. There is a pizzeria on the first floor and the Tavern Bar serves good pub food with an excellent selection of beers, wines and spirits.

TO GET THERE: The Dickens Inn is at St Katharine Dock, downstream of the Tower of London. Nearest station: **Tower Hill**.

The Town of Ramsgate, Wapping High Street

The Town of Ramsgate is a fine riverside pub. It has stood here, near to the former main entrance to London Dock, for many years. As far back as the fifteenth century there was a pub on the site, known as the Hostel, which then became the Red Cow, a reference, it is said, to a barmaid. It took the name Ramsgate Old

Town in 1766 and its present name in 1811, alluding to the Ramsgate seamen who used to land their fish at Wapping Old Stairs next to the pub.

It was here, so the story goes, that the notorious judge, George Baron Jeffreys, was captured disguised as a sailor, trying to flee the country on a German ship. He foolishly went ashore and it was at Wapping Old Stairs, next to The Town of Ramsgate, that Jeffreys was recognised by a scrivener, whom the tyrannical judge had once prosecuted. Taken to the Tower of London, Jeffreys died in 1689. His sticky end was foretold, in a way, by his father who, when Jeffreys was a young man, predicted he would come to a violent end. His father wanted him to enter a quiet and respectable profession, but Jeffreys sought advancement through the law. Despite being described by Charles II as having 'no learning, no manners and more impudence than ten carted street walkers', he was appointed

Wapping Old Stairs, by T. Rowlandson.

Lord Chief Justice in 1683. Jeffreys, the 'hanging judge', rose to even greater rank as Lord Chancellor under the Catholic James II. Protestant discontent had encouraged the Duke of Monmouth, illegitimate son of Charles II, to land at Lyme Regis and press his claim for the throne. He was proclaimed king by his supporters at Taunton, but was defeated by King James's forces under John Churchill (later made 1st Duke of Marlborough) at Sedgemoor. Jeffreys dealt with the rebels in a most brutal way at the infamous 'Bloody Assizes' – 200 were hanged and 800 were transported to the colonies. But the Glorious Revolution of 1688 brought an end to the reign of James II and with it his Lord Chancellor.

The Town of Ramsgate is a Grade II listed building with a fine beamed ceiling, benches, plank panelling and engraved glass screens. Good traditional pub food is served, with roasts on Sunday. A choice of cask ales can be enjoyed while admiring the river view from a small seating area.

TO GET THERE: Turn left from **Wapping station** and walk along Wapping High Street for 300 yards.

The Captain Kidd, Wapping High Street

The Captain Kidd pub is a little further east from The Town of Ramsgate. It is a splendid pub, with excellent river views throughout, especially from the outdoor terrace, but is not ancient, dating from a warehouse conversion of the 1980s. There is a restaurant available and Sam Smith's beer is served. Adjacent are two eighteenth-century houses typical of those that were here before the docks arrived. Nearby is the site of the notorious Execution Dock,

The Captain Kidd, Wapping.

where pirates were hanged for their crimes as late as 1830. Stow tells us it was 'the usual place for pirates and sea rovers, at the low-water mark, and there to remain till three tides had overflowed them'. One to lose his life here was the famous buccaneer, Captain Kidd. Born in Greenock on the banks of the Clyde, Kidd was the son of a clergyman. He fought for William III against the French and was often in the New World. It was the colonial governor of New York who persuaded William III to commission 'our trusty and well-beloved Captain Kidd' to search for pirates off the coast of Africa. Kidd set off in his ship, the *Adventure*, but try as he would, he found none – and this, of course, meant that his voyage was in danger of becoming a financial failure.

With a mutinous crew – whose income depended on capturing ships – demanding he be less rigorous in his choice of targets, Kidd crossed the line into piracy, and soon had the Royal Navy chasing him. He was eventually arrested in Boston, New England, in 1699, and thrown in gaol for a year. Sent back to London, he was accused of murdering one of his crew by striking him with an iron-bound bucket. Kidd protested that the man had been mutinous – making his killing legal – but to no avail. In 1701, he was found guilty of murder and piracy. Suspicion surrounded his trial, given that the only evidence against him was provided by two crew members of the *Adventure*. Nonetheless, he was hanged at Execution Dock in front of a large crowd, including one of his mistresses. When he saw her, Kidd shouted, 'I have lain with that bitch three times and now she has come to see me hanged.' He is reputed to have buried his ill-gotten treasure, and after a haul was found off Long Island, New York, fortune-hunters continued to search the Hudson River in the hope of finding more. Kidd was an inspiration for Robert Louis Stevenson's *Treasure Island*, and his exploits were featured in a film starring Charles Laughton.

TO GET THERE: Turn left from **Wapping station** and walk along Wapping High Street for 100 yards.

Prospect of Whitby (Glamis Road/Wapping Wall)

The Prospect of Whitby dates from the 1520s, when it was a country house; it soon became an inn known as the Devil's Tavern – a reference to the nature of its customers, who tended to be smugglers and thieves. It took the name Prospect of Whitby in 1777, after the coal ship *The Prospect*, registered at Whitby in North Yorkshire, which often moored near the tavern. Samuel Pepys was an early customer, and it is claimed that Dickens, Turner, Whistler and Gustave Dore later supped here. It became fashionable in the 1960s with those from the West End who sought a slice of East End life, Rod Steiger and Paul Newman included. There are splendid river views from its bars.

TO GET THERE: Turn right from **Wapping Station** and right at Wapping Wall for 200 yards.

The Narrow (Narrow Street, Limehouse)

The Narrow is a gastropub and part of the Gordon Ramsay group. It sits in an enviable position at the entrance to Limehouse Basin and there are excellent views of the river as well. The pub used to be called the Barley Mow before Ramsay bought it and before that it was the Regent's Canal Dockmaster's House.

TO GET THERE: From **Limehouse DLR** walk down Branch Road (to the left of the entrance to the Rotherhithe Tunnel); at the T-junction turn left, then right to arrive at Narrow Street where turn left to the pub at the entrance to Limehouse Basin.

The Grapes (Narrow Street, Limehouse)

The Grapes, Narrow Street, Limehouse.

Dickens often visited his godfather in nearby Newall Street. He must have known The Grapes and it is thought that this pub is his 'Six Jolly Fellowship Porters' of *Our Mutual Friend*, although the nearby, but now long gone, Two Brewers is another contender. The timber balcony at the rear has views over the river, with a restaurant upstairs serving great pub food and a real pub below. Jerome K. Jerome, well known for his love of the Thames, lived nearby and was likely to have been familiar with The Grapes. Dickens described it as:

A tavern of dropsical appearance … long settled down into a state of hale infirmity. It had outlasted many a sprucer public house, indeed the whole house impended over the water but seemed to have got into the condition of a faint-hearted diver, who has paused so long on the brink that he will never go in at all.

The Grade II listed Grapes is part owned by Sir Ian McKellen, features in the *Good Pub Guide* and dates from 1720, although there has been a pub on this site since 1583. The artist Francis Bacon lived and worked nearby at No. 80 Narrow Street, Edward Wolfe at No. 96. On The Grapes' walls are oil paintings by the marine artist Napier Hemy, watercolours of Limehouse Reach by Louise Hardy and *Dickens at The Grapes* by the New Zealand artist Nick Cuthell. Opposite is Jane Ackroyd's sculpture *Herring Gull* at the head of a charming open space. It was here that Roy Jenkins, David Owen, Shirley Williams and Bill Rogers, otherwise known as the 'Gang of Four', gave birth to the Social Democratic Party in 1981, with their 'Limehouse Declaration'. Next to The Grapes is a clean elegant row of Georgian houses, the earlier ones differentiated by their windows being flush with the wall. There were once shops in their ground floors.

TO GET THERE: From the Narrow (see above) continue for 150 yards. Alternatively, from **Westferry DLR** walk westwards along Limehouse Causeway, soon becoming Narrow Street, for about 400 yards.

The Gun (Coldharbour, off Preston's Road)

The Gun used to be a working-class dockers' boozer. It is now a Fuller's gastropub. The pub has a long association with smugglers landing contraband on the site and distributing it via a hidden tunnel. To this day there is a spyhole in the secret circular staircase that was used as a watch out for 'The Revenue Men'. The Gun is an eighteenth-century Grade II listed building and has

The Gun, Isle of Dogs.

excellent views over the river to the O2 Arena.

There is a tradition that Horatio Nelson stayed at what is now Nelson House and visited Lady Hamilton at The Gun public house, allegedly entering via the secret tunnel. There has been an inn on the site since the fifteenth century. It was known first as the King and Queen, then the Rose and Crown, then the Ramsgate Pink. The present pub takes its name from the guns that blazed forth from the *Henry Addington*, the first ship to sail into the West India Dock.

TO GET THERE: Turn right from **South Quay DLR** along Marsh Wall, at the end turn left into Manchester Road, cross the Blue Bridge and first right.

The Ferry House (Ferry Street, Isle of Dogs)

The Ferry House is an old established pub serving good ale and good cheer. It serves as a reminder that the ancient Potter's Ferry ran from nearby, to and from Greenwich, carrying 'men, horses, beasts and all other cattle'. In the late nineteenth century, a steam ferry ran every twenty minutes for a 1*d* fare. But in 1902, the Greenwich Foot Tunnel opened and this spelled the end for the ferry. The pub itself dates from about 1740.

TO GET THERE: Turn right from **Island Gardens DLR** for 200 yards and then left at Ferry Street.

The Great Eastern (Saunders Ness Road, Isle of Dogs)

This listed pub used to be called the Newcastle Arms until it was renamed the Waterman's Arms in the 1960s by the landlord, Dan Farson. It is now the Great Eastern. Under Farson, it enjoyed a period of some considerable fame with groups from Kensington and Chelsea coming to 'do the East End'. As early as 1978, Sir Geoffrey Howe suggested, during a Bow Group dinner

The Great Eastern, Isle of Dogs.

in the pub, the idea of 'enterprise zones' to regenerate the redundant dock areas. Farson gave the pub an 'old time' music hall atmosphere and put on an exhibition of portraits by Stephen Ward, the osteopath involved in the Profumo scandal. There have been many famous celebrities who have visited, including Francis Bacon, Sarah Vaughan and Shirley Bassey.

TO GET THERE: Turn left from **Island Gardens DLR** for 200 yards, then right along Glenaffric Avenue.

Ship and Whale (Gulliver Street, Rotherhithe)

The aptly named Ship and Whale is tucked away near to the riverside end of Greenland Dock. It is at the end of Randall's Rents, the narrow walkway that was used a passage for dockworkers to get from their homes to work. First built by local shipwright John Wells in 1698, Randall's Rents was originally called Wet Dock Lane. The name was later changed to Randall's Rents, after the famous shipyard, which towards the end of the eighteenth century was one of London's largest, constructing sailing ships for the East India Company and early steam-powered vessels. The pub has a pleasant garden backing onto Odessa Wharf, which was built as a granary in the nineteenth century and is now converted to timeshare apartments. The pub first appears in the rate records of 1767; however, the present building is believed to have been rebuilt around 1880. There are craft beers, superb homemade food and a great atmosphere.

TO GET THERE: Take the C10 bus and alight at Surrey Docks Farm, continue south along Rotherhithe Street, turn left into Odessa Street and continue ahead.

The Mayflower, Rotherhithe (Rotherhithe Village)

An ancient milepost outside tells us it is 2 miles to London Bridge. The pub was originally known as The Shippe and later The Spread Eagle and Crown but was renamed, for obvious reasons, in 1956. The pub is a firm favourite of mine and still sells stamps from both the USA and UK; this unusual custom came about because it gave seamen coming ashore, with little time to spare, the opportunity to buy stamps. The *Mayflower* was a Rotherhithe ship and it was from Rotherhithe that Captain Jones set off for Southampton and Plymouth and from there to America. There is a balcony at the rear where you can enjoy your pint of beer, admire the fine river views and call to mind Christopher Jones and the brave pilgrims, who some claim left from this very spot. The pub has a special book, the Mayflower Descendant's Book, which can be signed by anyone who can prove family connections with the Pilgrim Fathers.

The pub serves excellent food, with a special pie day on Wednesdays and fish on Fridays.

Near the Mayflower is Rotherhithe Picture Research Library, housed in Grice's Granary. The Picture Library is open to all who wish to carry out research and covers a very wide range of subjects. Grice's Granary dates from as far back as 1796 and is one of the oldest in Rotherhithe. It is well worth inspecting from inside, where there are timber floors, 'hanging knees' of timber to support the ceiling and a kingpost roof.

TO GET THERE: Turn right from **Rotherhithe station** along Brunel Road. Turn right at Rupack Street and right again at the Ship pub. At the church, turn left. The Mayflower is ahead.

The Angel, Rotherhithe

Views from this well-known riverside pub must rank alongside the finest in London, with Tower Bridge to the west and Canary Wharf downstream. A pub has been on the site for many years and it claims many illustrious visitors, including Captain Cook, Samuel Pepys and the notorious Judge Jeffries, whose ghost still haunts its bars.

The Angel, Bermondsey.

Almost opposite The Angel is a rare find – the remains of a medieval manor house, built in the reign of Edward III. Discovered in 1902, when a commercial warehouse was being built, it was excavated in 1985. The house was built around two courtyards. Edward III stayed here on occasions and resided in the northern and innermost courtyard. There was also an apartment for his son,

Prince Edward, the Black Prince. Edward III extended the house in 1353, at which time additions were made to house his falcons. In 1361, the manor house was described as having a hall, kitchen, chambers, a gatehouse and garden. After Edward's death it was successively owned by St Mary Graces and Bermondsey Priory. After the Dissolution, it passed to a number of owners including Peter Hills, who founded a school in Rotherhithe opposite the parish church. In the mid-seventeenth century pottery was made here, after which the site was occupied by an engineering works, granary, tobacco warehouse and even a police station.

TO GET THERE: From **Bermondsey Jubilee Line** station turn right along Jamaica Road for 300 yards, then left along Cathay Street. The Angel is ahead.

King Edward III Manor House, Bermondsey.

SOURCES OF REFERENCE

S.K. al Naib and R.J.M. Carr, *Dockland: An Illustrated Historical Survey of Life and Work in East London* (North East London Polytechnic, 1986).

J. Bird, *The Geography of the Port of London* (Hutchinson, 1957).

H. Bloch, *Newham Dockland* (Chalford, 1995).

M. Boast, *The Mayflower and Pilgrim Story – Chapters from Rotherhithe and Southwark* (London Borough of Southwark, 1970).

M. Boast, *The Story of the Borough* (London Borough of Southwark, 1982).

M. Boast, *The Story of Bermondsey* (London Borough of Southwark, 1998).

Sir J. Broodbank, *History of the Port of London* (Daniel O'Connor, 1921).

I. Butler, *Murder in London* (Robert Hale, 1973).

P. Colquhoun, *Treatise on the Commerce and Police of the River Thames* (1880).

I.D. Colvin, *The Germans in England* (National Review Office, 1915).

J.E. Connor, *Stepney's Own Railway: A History of the London & Blackwell System* (Connor and Butler, 1984).

J.E. Connor, *Branch Lines Around North Woolwich* (Middleton Press, 2001).

G.R. Corner, *History of Horselydown* (Cox & Wyman, 1858).

B.H. Cowper, *History of Millwall, Commonly Called Isle of Dogs* (Robert Gladding, 1853).

J. Cox, *London's East End* (Weidenfeld and Nicolson, 1994).

Arthur Philip Crouch, *Silvertown and Neighbourhood* (Thomas Burleigh, 1900).

Kevin D'Arcy, *London's 2nd City, Creating Canary Wharf* (Rajah Books, 2012).

M. Darby, *Waeppa's People* (Connor and Butler, 1988).

A. Douglas, *Current Archaeology*, 193 (2004), 20–27.

R. Douglas Brown, *The Port of London* (Terance Dalton Ltd, 1978).

C. Ellmers and A Werner, *Dockland Life: A Pictorial History of London's Docks, 1860–2000* (Mainstream, 2000).

M. Essex-Lopresti, *Exploring the Regent's Canal* (Brewin, 1994).

H. Finch, *The Tower Hamlets Connection* (Tower Hamlets Library Service and Stepney Books, 1996).

J. Foster, *Docklands, Cultures in Conflict, Worlds in Collision* (UCL Press, 1999).

Simon Garfield, *Mauve* (Faber & Faber, 2000).

I.S. Greeves, *London Docks 1800–1980* (Thomas Telford, 1980).

Josiah Griffin, *History of Surrey Commercial Docks* (British Library, 1877).

G.N. Hardinge, *The Development and Growth of Courage's Brewery* (Jordan-Gaskell Ltd, 1932).

S. Harrison and S. Evemy, *Southwark: Who Was Who* (London Borough of Southwark, 2001).

Eve Hostettler, *Shipbuilding & Related Industries on Isle of Dogs, in Dockland, an Illustrated Historical Survey of Life and Work in East London* (North East London Polytechnic, 1986).

J. Hovey, *A Tale of Two Ports, London and Southampton* (Industrial Society, 1990).

S. Humphrey, *The Story of Rotherhithe* (London Borough of Southwark, 1997).

Alan Jackson, *London's Local Railways* (David & Charles, 1978).

Eric Kentley and Robert Hulse, *Brunel's Great Eastern* (The Brunel Museum, 2016).

Eric Kentley, Robert Hulse and Julia Elton, *Brunel's Tunnel* (The Brunel Museum, 2016).

John McIlwain, *HMS Warrior* (Pitkin, 1991).

Colin Manton and John Edwards, *Bygone Billingsgate* (Phillimore, 1989).

P. Marcan, *Bermondsey and Rotherhithe Perceived* (1998).

Geoff Marshall, *London's Industrial Heritage* (The History Press, 2013).

A. Mathewson and D. Laval, *Brunel's Tunnel and Where It Led* (Brunel Exhibition, Rotherhithe, 1992).

Kit Mayers, *Stephen Borough and the First Tudor Explorations* (Sutton, 2005).

G. Milne, *The Port of Roman London* (Batsford, 1985).

G. Milne, *The Port of Medieval London* (Tempus, 2003).

G. Milne, *Current Archaeology*, 6 (1979), 198–204.

G. Milne and D. Goodburn, *Antiquity*, 64 (1990), 629.

G. Milne, R.W. Batterbee, V. Straker and B. Yule, *London and Middlesex Archaeological Society*, 34 (1983), 9–30.

Newham (Background to the Borough), *Local History Publication No. 1* (London Borough of Newham, 1972).

Lauren Paine, *Captain John Smith and the Jamestown Story* (Robert Hale, 1973).

M. Paris, *Silvertown 1917* (Ian Henry Publications, 1986).

J. Pudney, *London's Docks* (Thames and Hudson, 1975).

S. Rankin, *Shipbuilding in Rotherhithe – An Historical Introduction* (Dockside Studio, 1997).

S. Rankin, *A Short History of the Surrey Commercial Docks* (Dockside Studio, 1999).

S. Rankin, *Shipbuilding in Rotherhithe – The Nelson Dockyard* (Dockside Studio, 1999).

D. Rimel (ed), *A Trail Walk Around Old Rotherhithe* (Time and Talents Assoc., Rotherhithe, 1994).

L. Roche, *Butler's Wharf – A Brief Social and Economic History* (1984).

The Royal Mint — An Outline History (HMSO, 1967).

H. Spencer, *London's Canal* (Putnam, 1961).

C. Stansfeld Hickes, 'Shipbuilding on the Thames', *P.L.A. Monthly* (1927), 131 & 219

C. Stansfeld Hickes, 'Shipbuilding on the Thames', *P.L.A. Monthly* (1928), 79 & 361

Survey of London: Poplar, Blackwall and the Isle of Dogs, XLIII, XLIV (1994).

Rosemary Taylor and Christopher Lloyd, *The East End at Work* (1999).

Gilbert Torvy, *The Book of Queenhithe* (Barracuda Books, 1974).

John M. Thompson (ed.), *Journals of Captain John Smith* (National Geographic, 2007).

Taliesin Trow, *Sir Martin Frobisher* (Pen & Sword, 2010).

Various Authors, *Perkin Centenary London, 100 Years of Synthetic Dyestuffs* (Pergamon, 1958).

W. Vaughan, *On Wet Docks, Quays and Warehouses for the Port of London, with Hints Respecting Trade* (1793).

R. Vickers and D. Perrett, *Industrial Archaeology Walks in London – Southwark: Tower Hill to Rotherhithe* (GLIAS, 1984).

A. Vince, *Saxon London* (Seaby, 1990).

J. Watson and W. Gregory, *Free for All* (London Borough of Greenwich, 1986).

B. Weinreb and C. Hibbert (eds.), *The London Encyclopaedia* (Papermac, 1983).

S. Williams, *Docklands* (Architecture Design and Technology Press, 1990).

E. Williamson and N. Pevsner with M. Tucker, *The Buildings of England: London Docklands* (Penguin Books, 1998).

J. Willis, *Extending the Jubilee Line* (London Transport, 1999).

Lady Yarrow, *Alfred Yarrow: His Life and Work* (Edward Arnold, 1923).

Websites

Tate & Lyle: www.tate-lyle.co.uk
London City Airport: www.londoncityairport.com
ExCeL: www.excel-london.co.uk
Canary Wharf: www.canarywharf.com
Royal Docks: www.londonsroyaldocks.com

INDEX